The *Pocket Scroll*® Series

SHAAR PRESS

Rabbi Zelig Pliskin

SELF-CONFIDENCE

Formulas,
Stories,
and Insights

published by

PocketScroll®

SHAAR PRESS

TABLE OF CONTENTS

INTRODUCTION

I have spoken to many successful people. Their self-confidence was the common denominator that enabled them to be successful. I have also spoken to many people who were not yet successful. They hadn't yet developed their unique self-confidence.

This book contains ideas and tools that have proven effective for a wide variety of people. It can help you build your self-confidence in your own way.

Self-confidence is a mental quality and a learnable skill that enhances every aspect of your life. Self-confidence enables you to utilize all of your knowledge, wisdom, skills, and talents to make and reach meaningful goals. With self-confidence you can think, speak, and act at your best, highest, and wisest.

With self-confidence you realize that you already have much knowledge and will be able to constantly gain more knowledge. You realize that you already have many skills and talents, which you can continue developing along with other skills and talents.

Self-confidence helps a person feel more comfortable in more situations. A person with modest self-confidence projects an attitude of competence and makes a better impression during interviews of all kinds. It is an asset when it comes to making friends and influencing people.

When speaking in public, a self-confident person more easily expresses ideas in a way that will be viewed favorably. All teachers are public speakers. A self-confident salesperson is more successful in selling and does not take a refusal to buy as a personal rejection. Anyone who needs to influence and persuade others is a salesperson. A parent is both a public speaker and a salesperson. Fathers and mothers speak to their children whenever they talk in front of their children. Fathers and mothers constantly sell their values and ways of being to their children of all ages.

A lack of self-confidence can be a major handicap in a person's life. It will prevent a person from being all that he could possibly be. The absence of self-confidence will give the impression that he doesn't know as much as he does and isn't as competent as he actually is.

A person who is self-confident will be in more resourceful emotional states than someone who lacks self-confidence. A lack of self-confidence causes a person to worry and experience higher levels of anxiety and stress. Lack of self-confidence goes together with a lower self-image and a lack of self-respect. Self-confidence leads to a calm state of well-being.

In *Building Your Self-image and the Self-image of Others* (ArtScroll, 2006), I elaborated on the concept of self-image and how to build it. Some people have a strong sense of their inner value as a person, but still lack self-confidence in various areas. This book is an antidote.

Some people are concerned that self-confidence may be considered arrogance or conceit. True humility, however, is an awareness that one knows what he knows and can do what he can do. But one appreciates that all his knowledge, skills, and talents are gifts from the Creator.

Realistic confidence helps a person move forward in life. Confidence without competence is a fault rather than a virtue. That is, a person who believes he can do something well but really can't, and won't listen to feedback, might make serious errors. But if a person is self-confident and open to feedback, he will be able to learn from each experience, viewing them as experiments, and he will eventually gain great competence.

A highly self-confident person isn't afraid to take sensible action and look for feedback: "Should I continue to do this and similar things, or is it better from me to say or do something else to reach my goal and get the outcome I want?"

Regardless of a person's present level of self-confidence, anyone can develop greater self-confidence. Some people view self-confidence as a trait that either one has or doesn't have, and think that there isn't much to be done about it. My experience has shown that anyone open to new ideas who is willing to apply the exercises in this book will be able to increase his level of self-confidence.

I have interviewed people who grew up with high levels of self-confidence and found out what thoughts and attitudes enabled them to have such self-confidence. We can all learn from them. I also interviewed people who started with lower levels of self-confidence and then, either by themselves or with the help of others, were able to gain greater self-confidence. This self-confidence enabled them to achieve what they would not have otherwise achieved while maintaining greater levels of well-being and inner calm.

Please note that the goal of this book is to serve as a tool to condition the reader's mind to increase self-confidence. The basic principles are quite simple, but many repetitions are needed for these ideas to become integrated and internalized. Sections might seem similar, but the slight nuances will have long-term benefits. Be patient. You are planting ideas and concepts in your mind. Just as a seed needs time to grow into a great big fruit-bearing tree, these words will eventually enable you to develop your unique self-confidence.

Intensify your desire to be self-confident. Don't just wish you were more self-confident, or waste time and energy complaining that you are not as self-confident as you wish you were. Read the ideas in this book over and over again. The neural pathways in your brain will develop like muscles that are exercised regularly. This actually creates a change in your brain and leads to greater self-confidence in thoughts, feelings, words, and actions.

Identify yourself as a person who is self-confident. If you can't sincerely say, "I am a person who is self-confident," it's great that you are about to read this book. As you make progress and begin to experience speaking and acting like a person who is self-confident, you will eventually be able to say, "I am self-confident," and your truth detector will acknowledge, "Yes, you are!" But even before this becomes your reality, you can honestly say, "I am a person who is in the process of upgrading my self-confidence."

It is a major act of kindness to help people increase their level of realistic self-confidence. I hope and pray that this book will find its way to people who will benefit. May you utilize your self-confidence to upgrade your life and the lives of many others.

• • •

I am extremely grateful to the entire ArtScroll staff for all they have done to publish this book and my previous ArtScroll books. I am especially grateful to Reb Shmuel Blitz.

I deeply appreciate Mrs. Tova Ovit's masterful and professional editing.

I am grateful to my dear friend Rabbi Kalman Packouz for his friendship and encouragement.

1

SELF-CONFIDENCE: IT'S ALL IN YOUR MIND!

Self-confidence is created and stored in your mind. What is wonderful about this is that your mind is always with you, day and night and in all seasons, wherever you go.

Everyone has moments of self-confidence. Some people have more of these moments and others not as many. But regardless of how self-confident one usually is on a regular basis, there are memories of self-confidence stored in every person's brain. This is true of every person alive. And it is true for you.

All your positive experiences of self-confidence are recorded in your brain. A computer stores many documents that can be accessed with the right key strokes. So, too, you can access the pictures and sounds and feelings of self-confidence that your phenomenal mental computer, known as your brain, has stored within. Whether you consciously remember them or not, the memories are there.

We all start out in life not being able to walk and not being able to talk. Fortunately, when we are at the age of learning to walk and talk, we don't evaluate our ability. Therefore we don't say anything to ourselves that will limit us and prevent us from learning these skills.

For instance, if we don't begin talking at the same age as other toddlers, or we don't pronounce our first words correctly, we don't say to ourselves or others, "I guess I'm not a walker or a speaker." And since we don't limit and block ourselves from learning these skills, we all learn them.

As we get older, we learn many more skills and gain a lot more knowledge. We are all confident about a great many things that we know and can do.

Self-confidence is an attitude. A self-confident attitude is made up of thoughts of self-confidence and the positive feelings that go with it. Lack of self-confidence is also an attitude. This too is made up of thoughts and feelings. It is totally self-created, although it might be based on statements heard from authority figures who could and should have said more beneficial statements.

Lack of self-confidence is created by counterproductive patterns of thinking. These thoughts are not based on objective reality, but the person thinks that they are true. The negative feelings that go with it, however, are real feelings. But the thoughts that create them are not based on reality. Once someone realizes this, his path to self-confidence is opened up.

People who consider themselves as lacking self-confidence really have memories of self-confidence stored in their magnificent brain. But since they don't consider themselves to be self-confident, they will more easily remember instances when they weren't self-confident.

This is similar to someone who has a tremendous library of valuable documents in his computer. But not realizing what he possesses, he doesn't utilize his great treasure. Someone who knows about those precious documents can reveal the treasure. Once he knows it's there, it's easy to access.

This book can't give you self-confidence – and it doesn't need to. You already have self-confidence stored within. If you already know this, great! If not, let these pages give you the good news.

You are already the owner of self-confidence. Claim your ownership. You don't have to travel to pick it up. It doesn't cost anything. It can be found in your brain and mind.

Say out loud (or to yourself with a loud inner voice): "I am the owner of a tremendous amount of self-confidence. I will keep gaining a stronger and greater awareness of how easy it will be for me to think, feel, speak, and act with self-confidence."

"I wish I wasn't so insecure," an 18-year-old fellow said to me. "My insecurity is so strong and so deep I don't think I'll ever overcome it."

"We could speak for a long time about why you feel so insecure, and that might be very pleasurable for you. It's great to be understood and acknowledged," I told this young man who attended a class I gave on building your self-image. "But right now I only have a few minutes. Would you prefer to devote this time to telling me your story, or for me to share with you what I consider the most important idea about self-confidence?"

The attendee said, "Well, I can share my story with many people and I already have. You sounded very self-confident about the theme of your class. I would greatly appreciate hearing what you have to say about self-confidence."

"That's a wise choice. When I started teaching many years ago, I wasn't as self-confident as I am now. I have focused on this subject for a long time. What has made a major difference in my life is the awareness that self-confidence is an attitude that everyone has the ability to master.

"Self-confidence, or the lack of it, is based entirely upon what is going on in your mind right now. We all have a stream of thoughts from the time we wake up in the morning until we fall asleep at night. We all have a brain that we carry with us all the time. "As long as we are alive we can hear ourselves thinking. People who habitually think thoughts of gratitude and appreciation will create a happy life for themselves. Unfortunately, many people instead habitually focus on what went wrong in the past and what might go wrong in the future and what they don't like about the present. They will be masters of mental misery.

"Since we are so used to our habitual thoughts, we think that this is our nature. But our habits of thought are just habits, just like any other habit that we might have. We have the free will to choose better thoughts. The Creator gave us the potential for total control over our own minds. Total control is an unrealistic goal. I personally don't have total control and neither does any regular human being. Therefore, set a realistic goal to make better choices about the thoughts your mind will dwell on.

"Remember times you felt self-confident in the past. Imagine having greater self-confidence in the future. And choose to speak and act with self-confidence more frequently. Every new moment of self-

confidence is added to your mind's mental library. The more frequently you are self-confident, the easier it will be for you to access this way of being in the future. How does this make you feel?" I asked.

"This gives me a lot of hope," the fellow said with a look of relief on his face.

"I'm writing a book on self-confidence right now," I told him. "I feel that the ideas I am writing about have strengthened my self-confidence. When the book is published, I hope that you will read it and continue to build self-confidence in your own mind."

2

EARLIER THOUGHTS ARE JUST HISTORY. IT'S HOW YOU THINK RIGHT NOW THAT MAKES A DIFFERENCE

People want self-confidence to feel good in the present and to feel good about themselves in general. Self-confidence will enable them to say and do positive things and to make a positive impression on other people. This can be especially important in various meetings. They want to have a positive influence on the lives of other people.

These are all valid reasons. The goal of this book is to help readers meet their wants and needs in these and similar ways.

Your current level of self-confidence might be great already. But it might not be as high as it will be when you finish reading and integrating the ideas mentioned here.

Reading this book implies that you would like to increase your level of self-confidence. What counts is the self-confidence that you think and feel right at this moment, in any present moment.

If you have not been satisfied with your level of self-confidence, realize that is only a thought about earlier self-confidence. It's how you think right now that makes a difference.

This last sentence is so important that I will repeat it: It's how you think *right now* that makes a difference!

So let's say that later today, or tomorrow, next week, or next month, you expect to encounter a situation and you want to have a high level of self-confidence during that encounter. Your thoughts at that present moment will be the key factor in how you think, feel, speak, and act at that time.

Of course your past has an effect. And sometimes it has a very powerful effect. But by reading this book, new concepts about self-confidence have entered your mind. After you finished reading, the ideas are stored in your subconscious mind forever, even if you don't consciously think about what you read. So you can choose to have a high level of self-confidence.

When you encourage anyone else to have a higher level of self-confidence and you believe in that person, your words enter that person's mind. From that moment on, your conversation is an integral part of this person's past.

And from that moment on, your history will include the claim, "I have added to my personal self-confidence and I have had a positive impact on the lives of others."

Thinking that you are limited by your history is just that: a thought. It's a thought about a thought. Your current, positive thought about your upgraded self-confidence can replace and override a needlessly limiting thought.

I was speaking to someone about elevating his level of self-confidence, and he was upset with me for doing so.

— 21 —

"There is tremendous power in prior conditioning," he said vehemently. "You are not taking that into account. I have very valid reasons for not having self-confidence. I had older brothers who made fun of me and told me that I was stupid and silly. They told me that I wouldn't amount to much. When you have older siblings putting you down so strongly, it's understandable that you have low self-confidence."

"Yes, it is very understandable. However, right now, it's not really because of what they said to you that stops you from having higher self-confidence. It's your personal thoughts about what they said to you. Right now you can choose to believe my positive view of you rather than their limited and mistaken view of you.

"Who has more knowledge about the possibility of raising self-confidence: those siblings, so many years ago, or me, right now?"

"It's obvious that my brothers were not experts on how self-confidence is formed and how it can be raised," the fellow said with a laugh. "But what they said to me over and over again had a strong negative effect on me."

"I'm sorry that happened. But right now you are much older than your siblings were when they belittled you. They didn't reflect your reality then. And their comments certainly don't reflect your reality now. Does this make sense to you?"

"It certainly does. I wish I would have realized then what I realize now," he confirmed.

"We all do," I commented. "But now let your present understanding be at the forefront of your mind. This will do wonders for your self-confidence."

3

CHANGE YOUR FOCUS

There is a common tendency for people to focus on what they don't want.

"I don't want to have a low self-image."

"I don't want to feel bad about myself."

"I don't want to be so unhappy and miserable."

Some people have been talking like this for many years. Their intentions are positive, but they are making a major mistake.

In my earlier books, I stressed that our mind focuses on the words we say. We need to focus on what we want to become.

So when it comes to self-image, "I want to have a positive self-image" is the focus that is wanted.

"I want to feel good about myself" is more productive than, "I don't want to feel bad about myself."

"I want to feel happy and joyful more often" leads us in a better direction than, "I don't want to be so unhappy and miserable."

Repeating that we don't have self-confidence, or that our self-confidence is low, directs our focus on what we don't want. Instead, when we say, "My goal is to continually keep upgrading my self-confidence," we are focusing on what we do want.

This mindset enables us to focus on our ideal way of being. It reinforces our positive message over and over again.

It doesn't take a lot of effort to change our focus and begin talking in terms of what we want. And as one begins to talk in the positive direction, the new focus fairly soon becomes a habit.

The question to always keep in mind is, "How do I want to be?"

Then let your words and your actions answer the question.

"I don't understand why I don't feel better about myself," the 30-year-old executive told me. "I've been in therapy for a long time with a highly trained professional. He got to the root of my main problems. It's because of my low self-esteem. We've had many sessions tracing my low self-esteem back to my parents, my teachers, and my many failures in life. Yes, I've been financially successful, but I'm always emotionally stressed. I think that when I become even more financially successful and can consider myself in the super-wealthy category, then I will overcome my low self-esteem. Meanwhile, can you give me a shortcut that might help me right now?"

I explained to him that he is not alone. There are many people who have a goal to overcome a lack of inner self-confidence by getting in touch with their distressful memories and their uncomfortable feelings.

I continued, "Let me ask you a simple question, 'How do you want to feel?'"

"That's easy to answer. I want happiness. Doesn't everyone? I want to feel good more often and I want to feel good about myself."

"Great! That's a sensible request. When you think about your bad feelings, how do you feel in the present?"

"I feel bad, of course."

"And when you imagine that you have mastered being appreciative and grateful for all the good things that have happened to you, how do you feel?"

"I feel good, of course," he said with a smile.

"What I am going to tell you is common sense. And the good news is that recent research into the brain and its biochemistry have shown that when you think positive thoughts, your neural pathways to those thoughts get wider and make it easier to think those thoughts again. Moreover, the endorphins produced by positive thoughts are the healthy chemicals the brain produces whenever you feel good because of grateful thoughts and kind actions.

"By focusing on the joy of being self-confident and on all the potential good you can do in the world, your brain appreciates it and make these patterns your automatic way of being.

"The Rambam in Hilchos Dei'os wrote many years ago that the way to overcome negative traits and patterns is to develop positive traits and patterns by doing positive actions over and over again. Modern research explains what is happening inside our brains when we do," I concluded.

"I have an insight," the fellow said to me. "Instead of thinking so much about how I don't want to be, I will make it a habit to think about how I do want to be. I feel so much better already, just from imagining how this will change my entire life for the better."

4

SETTING GOALS DEPENDS ON YOUR LEVEL OF SELF-CONFIDENCE

In "The Four for Transformation Program," I elaborate on the four factors that will transform a person's life. These are: 1. Your self-talk. 2. Your self-image. 3. Your goals. 4. Your traits and states. When you improve your self-talk, your self-image, your goals, and your traits and states, you change your entire life.

The first factor is your self-talk, which is what you say to yourself. It's impossible to completely eradicate negative and limiting self-talk, and it is not wise to set an impossible goal. But you do have the ability to continuously improve your self-talk. Talk to yourself in ways that increase your positive feelings and minimize your negative feelings. Talk to yourself in ways that keep developing positive character traits and minimize negative character traits. Talk to yourself in ways that bring out your best and inspire and motivate you to accomplish and achieve worthwhile goals.

(For more on the theme of self-talk, read *Conversations with Yourself* [ArtScroll].)

The second factor is your self-image. You create your self-image with what you say to yourself about your identity. It is how you answer the question, "Who am I?"

As you improve your self-image, your entire life changes. How you saw yourself when you were growing up is not a key factor in your current self-image. What counts is how you see yourself now, in the present. In the present moment you are reading this chapter, and that means that you are thinking about your self-image right now. Right now, see yourself as someone created in the image of the Creator. You are a child of the Creator. And He created this magnificent world for you to appreciate and be grateful for. When you keep your thoughts focused on the good, you will see yourself in a positive light and will be motivated to improve what you personally can do to make your world a happier and kinder place.

(For more on self-image, read *Building Your Self-image* [ArtScroll].)

The third factor is related to your goals. The first step in reaching important goals is to clarify them. Be clear about what you want to be, do, and have. Then you need the *ratzon*, the willpower, to take action to achieve your goals. "Nothing stands in the way of a strong will." We cannot take this literally, because there can always be obstacles. But with a strong will, you can overcome many of them. With a strong will and a deep desire to reach elevated, realistic goals, you will not let temporary defeat allow you to quit.

People with intense willpower can do things that people

with similar abilities but weaker *ratzon* won't even dream about doing. What one considers "possible" or "impossible" to achieve depends on one's strength of will.

The fourth factor includes your traits and your states. Traits are your patterns of thoughts, feelings, words, and action. You can make any positive trait an automatic habit by frequent repetition. A person who used to be very selfish can transform himself into an authentically kind person with multiple acts of kindness. A person who used to lack confidence and courage can transform himself into a highly self-confident and courageous person with many instances of purposely speaking and acting self-confidently and courageously.

Your states refer to your mental and emotional states at any given moment. Take, for example, a joyful or an unhappy state. When you are in a joyful state, you think, feel, speak, and act very differently from when you are in an unhappy state. Even people with the trait of unhappiness can sometimes be joyful. And even people with the trait of joy can sometimes be unhappy.

You create your mental and emotional states with your mind and your body. For example, to create more moments of joyful states, remember what you think about when you are in a joyful state. Set your posture and facial expression to mimic what you do when you are in a joyful state to create more moments of joyful states.

Your mind and body together create any state you are in. External factors might be more conducive for joy or for unhappiness. But when appropriate, you can change your state from negative to positive or unhappy to joyful in a moment. You can also change your state of self-doubt and self-limiting to a powerful state of self-confidence and courage by changing what is going on in your mind and mimicking your expression and your positive way of sitting, standing, and walking. The more frequently you access powerful states, the easier it will be for you to do this in the future.

(For information about how free will allows you to choose your traits and states in the present, read *Life Is Now* [ArtScroll].)

You reach positive goals with your positive self-talk, positive self-image, and positive traits and states. The more self-confident you are, the higher you can set your goals.

As you read this book, imagine what goals you would set for yourself if you would be in your ideal state of mind. Setting goals can be challenging because we are not always in our ideal state of mind. The good news is that this very moment you are engaged in reading how to improve your state of self-confidence.

Using your ability to remember your greatest moments of self-confidence, recall some moments when you felt very self-confident. With your ability to use your imagination, imagine yourself acting extremely self-confident in the future. Now give yourself permission to imagine being given the gift of super great self-confidence. Realize that the only limits to your imagination are the limits you put on yourself. This exercise will program and condition your mind to have greater self-confidence.

Make it a daily habit to imagine yourself having high levels of self-confidence.

Every time you actually speak and act with self-confidence, you will be doing it in that present moment. Immediately afterward you will have another memory of speaking and acting self-confidently, a memory stored in the magnificent storehouse of your brain. Acting and speaking with self-confidence enough times will make it automatic. Even before it is automatic, at any given moment you can choose to use your mind and your body in ways that enable you to access self-confidence.

Making and reaching meaningful goals in life transforms one's entire life. People who lack self-confidence tend to set small goals. They don't believe they are capable of striving for large goals. They won't set or strive for goals beyond their self-image. I have met many people with trivial and limited goals. It's a tragedy because they have the potential for much greater goals, but their lack of belief in themselves prevented them from doing what they could have done.

On the other hand, there are people who have set major goals and have reached them. As my great teacher Rabbi Gavriel Ginsburg used to say, "If you reach for the stars you might not reach them, but at least you won't get your hands in the mud."

Every major accomplishment on our planet was achieved by people who had the self-confidence to do whatever was necessary. As you read this book, you are benefitting from the vision of ArtScroll's publishers. Rabbi Meir Zlotowitz and Rabbi Nosson Scherman had a great vision and the entire world has benefitted from their self-confidence. I am personally grateful to them and their entire staff.

I am currently reading the biography ArtScroll published about the life and great achievements of Rabbi Nosson Tzvi Finkel, of blessed memory. The book details the awesome power of an American boy from Chicago who became the head of the Mirrer Yeshiva in Jerusalem. His tremendous willpower and spiritual self-confidence didn't allow the debilitating effects of 30 years of Parkinson's disease to stop him from awesome greatness.

5
YOUR SELF-TALK EITHER BUILDS YOUR SELF-CONFIDENCE OR LOWERS IT

We human beings talk to ourselves all day long. This is also known as "thinking." We keep a running commentary about a multitude of things each day. Right now you probably have some self-talk about your views on self-talk. What you say to yourself either adds to your self-confidence or it does the opposite.

If your self-talk tends to minimize or lower your self-confidence, right now you can choose to use better, higher, and wiser self-talk.

Just being aware of what you are telling yourself about your self-confidence can be very beneficial. If you already say things that are positive and helpful, you can choose to keep the same pattern. You can even improve your positive self-confidence with even greater self-talk about your self-confidence. It's been said that the only limit to our mind is the limit we arbitrarily put on ourselves.

Affirmations are powerful. They work for us or against us. Every statement we tell ourselves about who we are and what we find possible or impossible is really an affirmation. Positive affirmations build us. Negative affirmations do the opposite. So right now you can tell yourself a great affirmation: *I choose better, higher, and wiser self-talk each and every day.*

Let's repeat this self-statement: *I choose better, higher, and wiser self-talk each and every day.*

Every time you say this phrase, you strengthen the neural pathways in your brain that contain this sentence. Modern technology has shown that these biological "wires" get thicker and thicker with repetition, so you are actually adding to your brain when you repeat, *I choose better, higher, and wiser self-talk each and every day.*

Whatever your earlier self-talk sounded like before is irrelevant: it is now in the past. We have free will to make better and wiser choices only in the present moment. So be joyful that you are reading this and are thinking about changing your self-talk. The Creator has given you the free will to repeat, *I choose better, higher, and wiser self-talk each and every day.*

You can try these affirmations to build your self-confidence through self-talk:

- *I am committed to saying things to myself that will add to my self-confidence.*
- *I already have a lot of moments of self-confidence, and my goal is to have even more moments of self-confidence.*
- *The more frequently I say and do things that take self-confidence, the easier it will be for me to say and do even more things that take self-confidence.*

- If you said something to yourself that could lower your self-confidence, you can say: *I realize that I just said something to myself that wasn't consistent with improving my self-confidence. I am extremely happy that I recognize this. I will now say something that will add to my self-confidence. I keep adding to my self-confidence each and every day.*
- *The next time I am aware of an anti-self-confident statement to myself, I will go out of my way to say three statements that build self-confidence.*

You might want to ask others, "What do you say to yourself to increase your self-confidence?" You only need to ask people who will be open to the idea of sharing what they say to them-selves.

It would be a good idea to write down five positive patterns of self-talk that can help further the development of your self-confidence.

I gave a class on building self-confidence recently and a student came over to me after class and said, "I am self-confident about a number of things. But when it comes to my general way of being, I have to admit that I am stuck with feelings of inferiority. A number of people have told me that I have low self-esteem and that I need to build my self-esteem. Some have implied that this is hard work and that it will take a long time. What do you think?"

"I think that it's much better and wiser and more efficient to think in terms of building your self-image. This is a lifetime process of finding out more and more that we have awesome potential. It's been said that whatever a person's mind can conceive of and believe in, that person can achieve. Way back in 1937, Napoleon Hill wrote a book about his research that took more than 20 years to complete. He had

interviewed 500 of the most successful men in the United States. He found that anyone famous for accomplishing great things believed that he could achieve what he set out to achieve.

"He spoke about Thomas Edison, the inventor of the lightbulb, who had had only three months of schooling. That is, only three months of elementary school and then he dropped out. So how did he gain the knowledge that he needed to invent what he did? He kept learning from other people who had the knowledge he wanted for himself. Today there are a tremendous number of specialized books that can teach you whatever you need to know to enhance your life and accomplish your dreams."

I added, "Do you know a recurring pattern of people who had self-confidence? They would repeat positive suggestions to themselves about their goals and about their self-confidence."

"But I heard from a number of people that autosuggestion doesn't really work. And that it's silly to think that you can just repeat, 'Every day in every way I am getting better and better,' and really get better," the student argued.

I explained, "Every tool needs instructions for proper use. People who say that affirmations don't work have given themselves an affirmation that did not work. Telling themselves that affirmations don't work prevented positive affirmations from working for them.

"The main reason that some people fail when trying to give themselves positive affirmations is that they don't keep it up long enough. They give up too easily. And as the saying goes, 'Winners don't quit. And quitters don't win.'

"In order for an affirmation to be effective, you need to repeat it with feeling and emotion. Those who repeat affirmations with a total *sense of belief that it will work, and repeat it with a powerful and upbeat tone of voice, have transformed their lives with positive affirmations.*

"To prove that something does work you only need a few examples. Really all you need is one example. But to prove that something doesn't work, you need 100 percent success at failing to work. And I know from my own experience that affirmations do work and that positive self-talk is a skill that can be learned," I concluded.

I saw from the look on the fellow's face that he was convinced. A follow-up telephone call confirmed that he was practicing positive affirmations about his self-talk, and that he was happier and more self-confident than he had ever been before.

6

YOUR MIND IMPACTS EVERY EXPERIENCE

We all have a constant flow of thoughts and mental pictures in our minds. These mental creations have a tremendous impact on how we feel, what we say and how we say it, and what we do and don't do. Some people are more consciously aware of this mental activity and its results.

People who are self-confident have very different mental pictures and thoughts than people who lack self-confidence. People who feel very insecure feel that way because of what they say to themselves and what they picture about the past and the future. When they change their self-talk and their mental images, they experience life very differently.

If someone says, "It's all in your mind!" as a way of not taking someone's distress seriously, of course it can be highly annoying. But imagine a compassionate and wise person gently and encouragingly telling someone that what he is experiencing is all in his mind. And then he explains kindly and patiently that we all have mental pictures and self-talk every moment of our lives.

When you can do something constructive to change an external situation, do so. However, if you can't or it will take way too much time and effort, then you can change your personal experience of what is happening by changing the way you think about the event.

Everyone who gains this awareness benefits in his own way. What this knowledge will actually mean to you will be unique to you. But the emotional improvement will make it much easier to have a more consistent level of self-confidence.

As you read this, you might have a deep understanding of how changing your self-talk and mental images can improve your life. Or you might already have a great awareness of this, and this chapter will just reinforce what you already know and understand. I personally find that being conscious of the concept is beneficial, even though I have already heard it many times and I have taught it to others.

When you are alone or not engaged in conversation with anyone else, you are engaged with conversations with yourself. These are the pictures and thoughts that are playing on the screen of your mind. Realizing that you can choose the next audio or video on this mental screen gives you tremendous power to create yourself in your ideal way of being.

Masters of self-confidence either have the ability to spontaneously change their mental "playlist," or they decide to see and hear themselves being self-confident. Right now, you too can choose to see and hear yourself being self-confident. It's up to you at any given moment.

An elderly person once told me, "I wasn't very successful in school. I was told many times that I wasn't trying hard enough. But I really was. I just thought that I was stupid and there was nothing I could do about it. But in high school one of my teachers said something to me that changed my life.

"He told me that he was able to become a teacher because one of his teachers had told him that being able to mentally see the words on a page is really a learnable skill. Most people look at a photographic memory as a gift that some people have and some don't. But once you realize that this is a skill you can pick up and gain expertise in, it becomes easier to access your mental pictures of what you studied. I didn't really believe him at first, but I trusted him and this gave me a lot of hope. Eventually I too was able to visualize the pages that I learned. I used to pretend that I could take a mental picture of the pages of the text that I studied. I was able to recall what we had studied in school. My marks on tests became better and I began to love learning new things," he concluded.

I pointed out that more and more children are realizing that they can mentally picture the words on a page. Expert spellers do this automatically. People who have difficulties with spelling can turn their eyes to look up to the right or to the left and can gain this skill.

Just as we can see pictures of the words on a page when we are no longer looking at the page, so too we can access the mental pictures of our good experiences to gain greater confidence in many areas of life.

7

FIGMENTS OF YOUR IMAGINATION

Years ago I met an ordinary fellow who had tremendous self-confidence. He was never intimidated by anyone. He was very likable and cheerful. He didn't get angry or upset by anything anyone said or did. He would just calmly negotiate workable solutions. Back then it didn't occur to me ask about his mental pictures and self-talk, but I eventually realized that something he had jokingly said a few times was the key to his unflappable inner calm.

He would say, "It's all a figment of my imagination."

Recently I remembered this and I finally understood. The idea of a figment of your imagination is like a cartoon character. It's not real. One can find it amusing, funny, humorous – but it's only imaginary. Every sane person realizes that if this character says something mean or cruel or "off the wall," there's no need to take it personally or seriously.

This gave him an extraordinary self-confidence. Others in his situation might experience fear or intimidation. But as long as the speaker wasn't actually dangerous, this fellow was unfazed by the angry voice. Regardless of how loud or offensive the remark, he just looked at it as a joke. He would be careful not to reply in a way that would give the speaker a reason to be violent. But inwardly he would dismiss what was said.

If the other person had a valid point, he would address the concerns. He would acknowledge the truth in what was said and correct what needed to be corrected. But he maintained his self-confidence.

Try using your imagination if you find yourself needlessly intimidated by someone's show of power or anger. You can say to yourself: "Right now this person is just a figment of my imagination. I will weigh what he says objectively. But I won't be intimidated. I won't say anything that will provoke this person. But I will maintain my self-respect and my dignity. I will treat this person with respect and compassion. But I will view anything potentially hurtful as if it was said by a cartoon character."

Someone who was easily intimidated by putdowns and insults told me that he was having a very difficult time with his employer. He liked his job, and his boss was pleasant when he was calm, but he had a short fuse and became angry easily. The boss returned to his pleasant self quite quickly, but what he said when he was angry lingered in this employee's mind. He would mentally repeat the boss's angry comments. Somehow the effects of the negative comments lasted much longer than the positive effects of what the boss said when he praised him. The boss had taken a course on how to get along better with other people and there he picked up the message of "Be hearty in your approbation and lavish in your praise." He did say a lot of positive things to his employees, but this did not stop him from insulting them when he lost his temper.

I suggested that the employee view his boss as if he was a funny-looking cartoon character whenever he became angry. Although he shouldn't show a lack of respect to a fellow human being, he would be smart to use his imagination to deflect the boss's angry outbursts.

He could even mentally play funny music to go along with the funny character. He could imagine an angry person having gigantic ears and a clown's nose. He could imagine that the person was wearing a ridiculous hat. Later on, instead of replaying the boss's actual words, he could imagine a ridiculous and funny tone of voice that would just make him laugh.

The employee started laughing and commented, "I never realized it could be so easy to transform a potentially distressful incident into a source of humor."

8

HAVE THE SELF-CONFIDENCE TO LEARN WHAT YOU NEED TO KNOW

Feeling self-confident is much easier when you are knowledge-able. When you know the necessary facts and figures, you feel self-assured. This feeling helps you to project an inner confidence that you have rightfully earned.

Someone cheerful, friendly, and honest about what he knows and doesn't know can self-confidently say, "I don't know the answer to that yet. And I will soon find out."

It's easier to have self-confidence if he already knows the information that is important for him to know. But he can feel self-confident even if he is not yet knowledgeable about a certain topic or subject.

Many people feel a bit uncomfortable if they don't know what they think they should know. They are embarrassed to say that they don't know. Some people might try to sound and act more knowledgeable than they really are. They try to guess answers, or even make up information since they lack the courage to say, "I don't know." They need the self-confidence to say, "I need to learn the answer and then I'll get back to you."

It is important to read books and articles on the topics that will have the most impact on your life. Many newspapers and magazines are filled with information that is not important. As you read this book right now, you are engaged in the process of learning about becoming more self-confident. This knowledge can be very helpful to you and to other people who will gain from your knowledge.

In school, the information with the highest priority should be the main things that are taught, but this is not always the case. You might have to do your own research to learn more about your own areas of interest.

Whenever you are able to, try to interview people who have the information that you would like to know. Enjoy the opportunity to quickly learn the information and insights that might have taken them a very long time to learn.

Thomas Edison had only three months of formal education. He dropped out of elementary school at a very young age. But he knew how to acquire the knowledge and information he needed in order to invent what he did.

An important question to ask knowledgeable people is, "What is important for me to know about this?" When you get into the habit of asking this question, you will find yourself automatically asking it whenever it will be beneficial to do so.

I spoke to someone who didn't do well in school. He managed to graduate high school, but he couldn't spell well and lacked much of the information that most people had. Nevertheless, he did very well in selling high-profit items. He was a person with integrity. His honesty and generosity earned him the respect of everyone who knew him.

I asked him how his lack of success in school impacted his self-confidence.

He laughed and told me, "I realized early on in life that it was much more important for me to be skilled at selling than it was to amass a lot of boring details about things I am not at all interested in. I was very respectful to my parents and knew how to win friends and influence people. This practical knowledge has enabled me to live a wonderful life.

"I have some friends who spent years working toward gaining diplomas and degrees. But they weren't as knowledgeable as I was about how to make money. I am much more self-confident about how to live a great life than they are. I use my money wisely and feel a great sense of accomplishment in helping so many people in so many ways. I was self-confident about myself as a child and easily maintain that quality now."

9

LACK OF SELF-CONFIDENCE CAUSES NEEDLESS HESITATION

Sometimes it is wise to stop and reconsider what you are about to say or do. By reflecting on the potential outcome, you might wisely decide that it's better not to say or do it. However, at other times, hesitating is caused by a lack of self-confidence. It would have been much wiser to simply take action.

It takes experience and wisdom to differentiate between positive and negative hesitation. According to our Sages (*Tamid* 32), the definition of wisdom is being patient and thinking clearly about the consequences of our words and actions. But hesitating because of a lack of self-confidence is not wise; it is a fault.

Hesitating has caused many people to "miss the boat," as it were. They miss out on great opportunities. Some opportunities are once in a lifetime. By building your self-confidence, you will be able to take advantage of opportunities that come along.

A word of caution: Some people have a tendency to hesitate

when they should have spoken up or taken action. Then they ruminate over and over how awful it was that they missed out on a wonderful opportunity. They keep repeating that they feel so miserable about not speaking up or not taking action. They overdo it.

The goal is a wise balance. Be aware of when insecurity is at the root of your hesitation. Build up your level of confidence. The next time something similar arises, take action. But don't allow yourself to be impulsive and to act prematurely.

It would be great to have a hard and fast rule to use as a resource for making the best decisions, but there is no rule. However, just knowing about positive and negative hesitation will help you gain greater clarity before you decide what to do. As you build your self-confidence, you will gain greater clarity as to whether it's best to hesitate or not in a given situation.

"I find it very difficult to make decisions," a 50-year-old executive admitted. "You might ask me how I manage without being a competent decision maker. The answer is that I rely on people who have a successful track record of making wise decisions. For example, when I was planning to buy my house, I had no idea if the purchase would be a good idea. But a very intelligent, trusted relative bought a house in the neighborhood and told me that it was a wise investment. If I wasn't satisfied, I could always sell the house at a profit.

"Some people try to make difficult decisions on their own. Their pride prevents them from consulting more knowledgeable people. I have the self-confidence to consult wise people and follow their advice. I am grateful to the Creator for giving me the wisdom of knowing who is wise."

10

MAKING THE
SELF-CONFIDENCE DECISION

I know people who consciously decided to be happy a number of years ago, and they have been happy ever since. Once they made that decision, they no longer asked each day, *Should I be happy today?* Of course, everyone faces challenges and on some days will feel better than others. When they come across a situation that used to bother them, they decide that it is not worth losing their feelings of happiness. Despite the everyday frustrations that cause many people stress, they are able to maintain their feelings of well-being. They are able to quickly bounce back and be resilient if they temporarily lost those feelings of well-being.

The same resilience applies to self-confidence. People who consciously decide to be self-confident are able to maintain their thoughts and feelings of self-confidence. This decision is not a vow or an oath. Rather, it is the awareness that everyone is entitled to a general state of self-confidence.

You can decide that from now on you will maintain a general state of self-confidence. This does not mean that you will never again feel insecure or a lack of self-confidence. But once you make the decision to be self-confident, you will experience this state frequently enough that it will be considered your normal and natural way of being. A young child can maintain a general feeling of self-confidence, even though he doesn't yet know many things and doesn't yet have many skills. But he doesn't tell himself needlessly limiting self-statements.

Some people doubt that they can maintain such self-confidence. But once they sincerely decide to make the self-confidence decision, it changed the way they saw themselves. They automatically dealt well with situations that used to be challenging for them.

If you decide to be self-confident, don't allow yourself to be frustrated and give up when you see that you're not in your usual self-confident state. The more frequently you are self-confident, the easier it will be for your mind to access this life-enhancing state.

I was coaching someone who told me that self-confidence was a constant struggle for him. When he felt self-confident, he was free from financial worries. He knew that he was talented and skilled enough to be of service to many people. But at other times he was overwhelmed with the worry of how he would support his family. When he felt optimistic, he thought of creative ideas and he was certain that they would work out. But when he felt pessimistic, he thought of all kinds of reasons why his plans would fail. He felt like a yo-yo going up and down in his levels of self-confidence.

"Describe how you think and feel when you are in your self-confident state," I said to him. "Tell me about some of the achieve-

ments you accomplished already and what you would love to accomplish in the future."

I saw his face become radiantly alive when he spoke of his empowered actions.

Then I asked him to describe what he thought and felt when he was in his pessimistic state. His face and his body took on the look of an old man. He lost his vitality and looked quite ill.

Then I once again asked him to describe how self-confident he was when he thought and felt optimistically, and I watched him come alive again.

Then I was able to point out to him, "Look at how easy it is for you to access your optimistic, self-confident state and then your pessimistic, insecure state. It's true that I suggested which states you should access. But you don't need me to do this.

"Make a strong and emphatic commitment to be self-confident. This decision will transform your life. You self-confidence will be much more consistent. You will accomplish much more and you will improve your day-to-day feelings. Does this make sense to you?"

"Yes, it certainly does," he agreed. "I never realized how easily I could do this. Right now, I hereby commit myself to choose to be self-confident regardless of external circumstances."

A follow-up discussion showed that he was able to maintain his self-confidence. His decision worked miracles for his life.

11

YOUR PERSONAL STORY ABOUT
YOUR SELF-CONFIDENCE

We all tell ourselves our life story. Even if a person doesn't consciously recognize that he is telling himself a story about his life, his life story has a major impact. Everyone's story about his life has major themes running through it. Some people have a highly spiritual life story. Some people have life stories about developing positive character traits while others don't. Some life stories are full of gratitude; others are not. Some life stories are full of happiness and joy; others aren't. Some life stories are concerned with major challenges and how they were dealt with wisely and with inner strength.

Even if someone isn't satisfied with his life story until now, he can choose to change the theme of his life story at any moment. It's never too late. Rabbi Avigdor Miller used to say that true success in life is recognizing the Creator. As long as one is still alive, there is an opportunity to pray to Hashem and connect with Him on a personal level.

This concept of our personal life stories applies to our thoughts about our self-confidence. What stories do you tell yourself about your self-confidence? Change the way you view your life story to improve your self-confidence.

Reading this book is a wonderful opportunity to add to your personal life story. As you read, visualize yourself continuing your life with greater self-confidence.

When you think about different situations that might arise in your life, see yourself thinking, speaking, and acting with greater self-confidence. These thoughts will lead to improved words and actions.

Pause if you ever catch yourself repeating the "I lack self-confidence" life story. Remind yourself that you have improved your thoughts about your own self-confidence. As you do, you will create many more positive self-confidence stories to add to your verbal autobiography.

"I heard that you are writing a book about self-confidence," someone said to me. "I would love to read your book. I know that my number one problem in life is that I lack self-confidence. I am insecure about who I am and what I can do with my life. Is there anything you can help me with even before I read your book?"

"The most important thing for you to realize is that you don't need anyone else to tell you what to do create more self-confidence," I replied. "What you tell yourself about yourself creates who you are. A person's self-talk and self-image are key factors in anyone's success in life or lack of success. Making worthwhile goals and believing that you can achieve them creates a successful life.

"Some people tell themselves stories of failure and of being a vic-

tim. Their tone of voice and posture is the opposite of what a person with a success story sounds and looks like.

"Start looking at your life as the great story of a great person. Many great achievers started off with humble beginnings. People respected and admired their heroic stories. Their stories are more dramatic exactly because they began with one failure after another."

I reminded him, "It's never too late to have a positive twist in your life's story. Now is a perfect time to change the tone of your life story. Just asking the question shows that you are ready for a positive change. Great!

"From now on, title your life story, 'How I raised myself to accomplish and achieve just by changing the title of my story.'"

"Wow!" he exclaimed. "I can feel the difference already. Yes, the title of a story makes all the difference in the world. I am totally committed to start a major rewrite of my life's story. The facts of the past are still the same. But instead of a woeful tale, I will transform it into the hero's journey."

12

SELF-CONFIDENCE TO ASK QUESTIONS

People with higher levels of self-confidence feel comfortable asking questions. People with lower levels of self-confidence might feel that they don't have a right to ask questions. They might worry that the person they ask might be critical of them for asking. Or they might worry about appearing deficient for not knowing the answers.

If a lack of self-confidence ever prevents you from asking a pertinent question, ask yourself, *If I had greater self-confidence, what would I ask right now?*

Then, even if you feel a bit uncomfortable about asking, realize you can speak up and ask. Once you do, you will have a breakthrough. You will have proven to yourself that feeling uncomfortable about asking a question doesn't need to stop you from asking.

It is usually easier to ask someone who is friendly, cheerful, and kind. You know that he will be happy to help you out and answer you. But you can imagine that anyone is really friendly, cheerful, and kind, deep down in his heart and soul. So when someone's attitude makes you feel a bit uncomfortable, imagine him behaving in an ideal manner and give yourself permission to ask your question.

If you are not certain how someone will respond to your question, you might want to explicitly ask, "Would it be all right if I ask you a question?" Most people answer, "Yes, it's fine."

Often, you can simply imagine that he gave you permission to ask. Ask yourself, *Do I have a right to ask this question?* If the answer is, *Yes. I do have a right,* then go ahead and ask. If the person really doesn't want to be bothered with your question, he will tell you so. We hope this person will eventually gain a greater level of patience and will appreciate doing the act of kindness of answering people's questions.

"In the areas that I am very interested in and that I do well in, I am highly self-confident and I also catch on very quickly," the fellow told me. "But in many other areas, I tend to feel tense and anxious if I don't catch on right away. It is difficult for me to stay calm and say, 'Could you please repeat that?' And if their repetition doesn't help me to understand, then I feel like saying, 'Could you please explain that in another way?' but I am too intimidated to ask for a clarification."

"I see that you know exactly what you need to say," I replied. "You just need to practice asking until you feel able to speak up. When you practice, don't imagine that you have to actually feel comfortable at first. All you need to do is practice enough times in the comfort of your own home, by yourself. With enough repetitions, calmly ask-

ing for clarification will become easier. Eventually you will have fun learning this new skill."

"Yes, I see now what I have to do. I used to view asking for clarification as something that's 'not my personality' and therefore impossible to do. I would be uncomfortable asking. But I'm realizing that feeling uncomfortable is not the same as impossible. There have been many things that I used to feel uncomfortable about that now I can easily do. I plan to make staying calm and asking questions another one of those things."

13

DON'T LET MORE KNOWLEDGEABLE, SKILLFUL, OR SUCCESSFUL PEOPLE LOWER YOUR SELF-CONFIDENCE

Your self-confidence is an inner attitude that depends solely on you. Self-confidence doesn't mean that you have to be smarter, more talented, skilled, or successful than any other person. When it comes to self-confidence, you are not in competition with anyone else. Even if someone else is more self-confident than you, his self-confidence has nothing to do with your self-confidence. Life is not a competitive sport. You don't need to outdo someone else to win in your "game of life." Life is not a race to see who is the fastest. Life is not a jumping contest to see who can jump higher. Life is a spiritual journey in which you connect with the Creator and your own inner spirit.

Some people feel they have a right to be self-confident only if they are better than others. But this is a myth. Regardless of where you are in your quest for knowledge and your level of any skill, you can have a general self-confident attitude. Self-confidence means that you are a person of infinite value. Your self-worth is never in question.

Your self-confidence is based on your own thoughts and feelings. And your thoughts are at the root of your feelings, your words, and your actions. Your self-confidence will be expressed by what you say and how you say it. Your self-confidence will be a resource for taking actions that will enhance your own life and the lives of others. Your self-confidence is totally independent of what anyone else thinks, says, or does.

Many people feel less self-confident around self-confident people who are more knowledgeable or skilled. It's not because of what the other person can do. It is because of their own thoughts about the other person's knowledge or skills. It's because of what they think about themselves when they needlessly compare themselves to another person.

Throughout life we gain more knowledge and increase the quantity and quality of our skills. As we practice any skill with conscious awareness, we improve the quality of that skill. We should avoid undermining our self-confidence by comparing our growing skills to those of people who have already improved their own.

Even if you have limited your own self-confidence for a very long time by comparing yourself to others, you can proclaim your mental freedom at any moment. Mental freedom from limiting oneself because of other people is a wonderful thing. Those who have realized this experience a deep sense of relief.

"Wow!" they exclaim. "I really can think and feel self-confident regardless of anyone else's self-confidence or achievements or potential!" You will benefit tremendously when you can think about this and internalize its significance.

It's similar to a person who was very satisfied with his own home for many years, until a wealthier person built a much larger and more expensive house nearby. If the person with the smaller house will focus on appreciating what he has, he can still maintain the same wonderful feelings about his own house. If, however, he continues comparing his own house in a negative way with the other person's house, he might feel totally deflated.

In reality, the size of his own house didn't change. Practically speaking, he can still enjoy his house in the exact same way that he always did. But his subjective level of appreciation will depend entirely on his own attitude.

An enlightened person will say to himself, *I am so happy for that other person. He must feel so great to have such a big house. He can do many acts of kindness for others. He has much more room for guests. He can invite many people to his home for meals on holidays and other festive occasions.*

But a person who is enslaved by thoughts and feelings of envy will lose much of his enthusiasm for what he himself has. He will feel bad that someone else has outdone him in his subjective race for having the best and largest and most expensive. He may lose a lot of his thoughts and feelings of self-confidence.

People who have the enlightened attitude are very fortunate. They have what it takes to be grateful, happy, and joyful. Even if someone doesn't yet have this attitude, he can spend time working toward acquiring it. This self-improvement costs less time, energy, money, and other resources than always trying to outdo someone else. It depends entirely on one's own thinking. True wealth is being joyful with what you have (*Pirkei Avos* 4:1). True poverty is feeling bad because someone else has it good. Be wise and be joyful. That is the true success in life.

I gave a class about how true freedom is freedom of the mind. An attendee declared, "I don't think you are right. Envy is a natural emotion and part of being human. I don't believe that anyone can overcome envy. Some might just deny their envy. But overcoming it? That's impossible."

This fellow was enrolled in a beginner's class on Torah values and character traits. He was so used to people being motivated by greed, honor seeking, and envy that he thought it was humanly impossible to transcend these attitudes.

"I can understand why you feel the way you do," I said. "I grew up in inner city Baltimore. But my father was a student of the saintly Chofetz Chaim in Radin. My father constantly spoke about his role model with great love and respect. Yes, we might be far from our greatest role models. But as a teacher of mine used to say, 'When you reach for the stars, you might not reach them, but at least you won't get your hands in the mud.'

"Perfection might be impossible. But free your mind by striving high and acknowledging your innate value and worth, with a deep sense of gratitude for everything you can be grateful for. This is a formula for a more elevated life."

14

YOU DON'T NEED TO FEEL SELF-CONFIDENT TO SPEAK AND ACT SELF-CONFIDENTLY

Your feelings determine whether you are experiencing happiness and joy or sadness and misery. Your thoughts, words, and actions create your feelings. When your thoughts, words, and actions are at their best, you will experience great feelings. Right now and every moment of your life, you have the free will to choose your thoughts, words, and actions.

Regardless of how you actually feel, you can choose to speak and act the way you would if you were feeling very self-confident.

Feelings are very important. But they are not the main thing. What you say and do with your life will make the greatest difference in who you are and what you accomplish. And people who think, speak, and act on a high level will usually feel accordingly.

But you can still speak and act self-confidently, even if you are not currently feeling self-confident.

Right now you can choose to speak and act in any way you desire. It's wonderful to feel the benefits of a self-confident attitude. But you don't need to be limited by a down mood or a negative state of mind.

It's possible to feel insecure yet act and speak with self-confidence. In my experience, when people consistently speak and act with self-confident patterns, they usually internalize the awareness that they are more self-confident than they feel. This realization gives us permission to actually feel the positive feelings of self-confidence.

I heard a definition of self-confidence as "feeling comfortable in one's skin." A person who feels comfortable in his own skin is not boasting or bragging and does not need external recognition of his abilities. He is not arrogant or conceited. Rather, he has a general feeling of well-being.

This isn't the same as a victorious prize fighter's feelings after winning a world championship boxing match. In reality, even the winner of a boxing match will feel a lot of physical pain. Those who look objectively at a professional boxing match will see the folly of two strong, grown men punching each other over and over. They are fighting like two young children who are angry at each other, for honor, applause, and financial gain. As Rav Noah Weinberg, of blessed memory, used to say, we see from professional fights the power of seeking glory.

When you are truly self-confident, other people's opinions do not change your level of self-confidence. You will be open to honest and authentic feedback but you won't take the feedback as personal criticism.

Actually feeling self-confident is valuable. But it's more important to choose to speak and act the way you would if you felt self-confident. With time, practice, and greater wisdom, a person who speaks and acts wisely will end up feeling accordingly.

An outreach yeshivah for people new to Torah Judaism was interviewing potential teachers. They sent a candidate to speak to me.

The candidate wanted a teaching job at the outreach yeshivah, but his mannerisms made him seem very unsure of himself. Both his tone of voice and his posture expressed a high level of insecurity. But when I spoke with him, his inner attitude was one of total confidence in his ability to teach and reach people on a deep level.

"I hear from what you are saying that you are really very confident about your abilities," I said encouragingly.

He confirmed, "I am. I know without a doubt that I will be a great teacher. I have a love for what I want to teach and I sincerely care about my potential students."

Although he felt confident, he didn't look or sound confident because of his tone of voice.

"This will be much easier than those who sent you to me thought," I reassuringly said to him. "You have a great attitude and you have a burning desire to be a great teacher. But right now you don't look or sound self-confident. I will demonstrate a posture you need to imitate and a tone of voice to emulate. Speak and act the way I will show you."

He was extremely open to changing his external patterns to match his inner self-confidence and passion for teaching.

"What did you do for him?" I was asked by one of the people who sent him over to me. "He looks and sounds like a different person."

Inwardly he was the same. But now his outer appearance gave the correct message. Similarly, an outer appearance of self-confidence can improve your internal self-confidence levels.

There are many people who are insecure and lack confidence. When they speak and act like a self-confident person and persist in mastering the skills and talents they want to develop, they will eventually feel, look, and sound self-confident.

15

POTENTIAL THOUGHTS

People with self-confidence are free to speak and act in ways that enable them to reach their potential. On the other hand, people who feel insecure and lack self-confidence might limit themselves greatly.

When a person lacks self-confidence, he might try to explain that he is being held back by his lack of education and knowledge, or his lack of family support, or his lack of finances, or his lack of a network of resourceful people. But in truth it's his thoughts about himself that are stopping him from fulfilling his potential.

Sometimes, external circumstances truly hold someone back from reaching his goals. What seems impossible is truly impossible. But achieving what is actually possible depends on one's thoughts, feelings, words, and actions.

One person might have less innate intellect and fewer talents and skills than other people. But thinking self-confidently and feeling self-confident will enable that person to utilize much more of the intellect, talents, and skills that he does possess.

No human being can know the full potential of another person. Nor can any human being know his own full potential. You don't need to know your full potential before starting to speak and act in ways that will enable you to reach more of your potential. You only need to take the next step forward.

You don't need to know your potential self-confidence before you begin to think, speak, and act with self-confidence. You only need enough self-confidence to take another small step. That makes the process sound much easier, doesn't it?

Needless limitations are all self-created by one's thoughts and feelings. This is also known as one's attitude. You can continue developing a more positive attitude. All accomplishments are achieved one step at a time. Keep moving forward by thinking, speaking, and acting in ways that will keep you in the right direction.

The words "the right direction" are very important words. When you are highly motivated to travel in the right direction, you will get much further. You know what the right direction means in your situation. Self-confidence is a key factor in not allowing negative thoughts to turn you from your path in the right direction.

A teacher, mentor, or coach is a highly valuable asset. Other people can make positive suggestions. They can tell you their best insights. But only you can think, speak, and act your way to becoming the best you that you can be. An inner drive to keep using more of your potential will help you get much further along.

Don't let your own thoughts needlessly stop you. With Divine assistance, your wise, self-confident thoughts can be your greatest ally in reaching your potential.

I knew someone who would frequently say, "I wish that I was smarter," "I wish that I was more talented," "I wish that I could accomplish more," "I wish that more people would help me out in more ways." He was always "wishing."

His wishes seemed to make sense. But as I got older I realized that his "wishing" was really holding him back. He was making a statement that only if his wishes would come true would he be able to achieve what he was put into this world to achieve.

The great spiritual teachers told their students, "You are only responsible for being the best that you can be. You don't need more intelligence than you have. You don't need a totally different emotional nature. You don't need to be someone else. You only need to be you. By authentically striving to be the best you that you can be, you will become exactly who you were put into this world to be."

16

"I CAN'T SEE MYSELF WALKING."

People sometimes claim that they aren't able to do something that they would like to do. They feel they are unable to do it. Even though they might believe they really can't do it, that belief is only a temporary mental limitation. Stating that they can't see themselves saying or doing something blocks them from improving themselves.

A small child who is too young to speak doesn't say, "I can't see myself talking." A young child who can't yet walk doesn't say, "I can't see myself walking." Their minds are not developed enough to think this way. They don't claim that since they can't see themselves doing something positive, they will never be able to do it. And then they learn to walk and talk.

A self-confident person knows that right now he can start making those mental pictures of success, even if he never before imagined himself saying or doing those things. Some people can see the mental images more clearly than others. But everyone can see themselves saying or doing anything that is positive to say or do.

Our minds create pictures of whatever we talk about. Some people have developed this ability and some haven't yet. But every little child can do this. You have mental recordings of yourself speaking and acting in various ways.

Visualizing yourself saying or doing something doesn't mean that you will actually do it. After all, using our great imaginations, we can see ourselves doing things that are humanly impossible to do! But declaring that something difficult is impossible brings a negative image to your mind. Instead, try to visualize yourself taking positive action to help make it a reality.

What would you love to achieve and accomplish? What would you feel great about doing with your life? What meaningful goals would you wish to reach? Imagine achieving and accomplishing everything that you would wish for. Picture yourself reaching your highest aspirations and your most meaningful goals. Visualize yourself speaking and acting the way you would with the highest and best character traits.

Practice seeing yourself saying and doing the greatest things. Practice seeing yourself accomplishing wonderful things. Practice seeing yourself achieving everything that you would wish to achieve. This visualization is a great step forward in building your self-confidence.

Your positive mental pictures help you do more. Positive mental pictures can help you overcome needless limitations. With positive mental pictures, imaginary blocks melt away.

Once you make it a habit to visualize yourself being the way you wish to be, you will find yourself actually speaking and acting in ways that are consistent with that ideal way of being.

An amazingly successful person once told me, "People wonder about how I became so successful. Some ask me for my secret. It's not really a secret. I appreciate the great gift of being able to imagine being any way I wish to be. I can imagine saying anything to anyone. I can imagine doing anything I need to do to reach meaningful goals.

"My mother used to tell me when I was a little boy, 'Use your imagination wisely. Don't use it to create needless worries and fears. Rather, imagine that you are super joyful just because you are alive. Imagine that you have all the courage you need to do anything great that you wish to do.'

"Other kids were smarter than I was, and more talented. But I excelled at utilizing my imagination. This has made me a fortune. But even more important: I became one of the happiest people that I have ever met. I imagine looking at myself in a mirror and smiling a great big smile. I don't even need a real mirror; I use the mirror in my mind.

"I imagine being a friend of other successful people. This has enabled me to build highly successful relationships with some great achievers who are mutually happy to have me as a friend. Imagination is the answer that people seek."

17

LOOKING THROUGH THE LENS OF SELF-CONFIDENCE

When a person looks through a colored lens, everything seems to be that color. If the lens is tinted yellow or blue, everything seems yellow or blue.

Seeing the world through rose-colored lenses also applies to our general attitude and frame of mind. A person who looks at life through the lens of gratitude will always find things to be grateful for. A person who looks at life through a mindset of anger and resentment will always find reasons to be angry and resentful. A person looking from a place of kindness and compassion will always find opportunities to be kind and compassionate.

If a person views life through the lens of insecurity, he will always feel insecure. Feeling insecure, he won't want to say or do anything that he considers risky, even in harmless, risk-free situations.

But if a person decides to view life from a place of self-confidence, this confident lens will color all that he sees. More positive opportunities will appear. He will be able to think of what to say and do in situations that an insecure mindset would avoid.

Seeing through the lens of self-confidence allows much more light in your world. A self-confident person sees further and clearer. The world appears totally different. Your outlook is so much brighter.

When you look through a strong telescope, faraway things seem much closer. Things that look tiny and small in the distance can appear much larger. When you realize that you have a right to see your life and your world through the lens of self-confidence, your vision will be greatly improved and more opportunities will be in your reach.

Ask yourself, *How would I view this person or this situation if I were seeing it from a perspective of self-confidence?* Use your ability to put on your self-confident lens. People who realized that they can switch lenses have found that suddenly they were able to think better, speak better, and act better. Perhaps changing your lenses will work for you too, so try it out and see.

I was giving a class on increasing our levels of happiness and building our self-image. Someone who hadn't heard me speak before challenged me and said, "You're making this sound too easy. It's easier said than done. I've wanted to be happier for many years and nothing has worked so far. I have a valid reason for not having a positive self-image. I've attended many seminars and have had many sessions with different therapists. What do you say to that?"

I replied, "First, I want to say that I'm sorry you've had many disappointments and have experienced so much distress. Please realize that I am not claiming that this change is easy or difficult. I'm just saying that it's possible to transform our lives when we upgrade our thoughts, words, and actions. Thinking that something is impossible makes it impossible for us. Thinking that something is possible makes it possible," I clarified.

"For instance, by challenging me, you have said something in front of others that many would not say. You have the self-confidence to speak up when someone says something that you don't agree with. Self-confidence is a great quality.

"To enhance your other qualities, imagine that you have a magic pair of glasses. These glasses let you see many things each day that you can be grateful for. Also, these glasses let you see many opportunities for kindness," I suggested.

"Next week I am giving another class. Please attend and report back to me how this idea has worked for you."

He realized he had nothing to lose and a lot to gain by trying it out. "It was unbelievable!" he reported the next week. "Trying on a new lens is such an easy concept. And it worked. I've felt a lot better this week than I have felt in a long, long time."

18
THE POWER OF "JUST FOR TODAY" AND "JUST FOR NOW"

Some people think it is too difficult to sustain a self-confident attitude over a long period of time. But many are willing to access their self-confident mindset for a short time, if they feel they are doing it "just for today," or "just for now." Deciding to improve "just for now" works for other positive traits, too.

People find it easier and simpler to accept a positive quality "just for today." This attitude does not mean they won't be self-confident tomorrow, too. They simply find it easier to improve without a long-term commitment to change.

Living one day with self-confidence seems less difficult than thinking that you need to be self-confident all the time. One day is much better than no days. So utilize this approach to improve your life one day at a time.

We live our entire lives one day at a time, one moment at a time. So if making a one-day commitment will work for you, then do it. And tomorrow you only need to make a commitment for that day. "One day at a time" thinking has helped people achieve great breakthroughs. Let it help you have greater self-confidence, one day at a time.

In the same way, "just for now" can help you have self-confidence for specific situations you find challenging. Having self-confidence "just for now" can get you through one encounter, meeting, occasion, or speech at a time. Again, we live our lives one moment at a time, regardless of how long we live. Many "just for now" moments add up. But in any given situation, you only need self-confidence "just for now."

People who have applied this "just for now" approach have found that after a few experiences their self-confidence has had such a boost that it's much easier for them to feel self-confident over and over again.

If you're not certain if you will have the necessary self-confidence when you need it in the near future, access your self-confidence "Just for now." You'll have an approach that you can try again and again for an unlimited amount of times.

"I have an interview coming up that is very important for my career," the caller said in a very worried tone of voice. "I feel certain that I will mess it up. This kind of thing always gets me very nervous. How can I change myself?"

"To totally change yourself might take more than just a single telephone call," I said to him. "But right now you don't need to totally change yourself. You only need to have enough self-confidence to become calmer and to think better during the interview," I reassured him.

— 74 —

I clarified, "Let's make it a lot easier for you. Just focus on having a sudden burst of inspired self-confidence for the duration of the interview. You don't need to know that you will always have self-confidence all the time, in every situation, for many years to come. You only need to feel calmer and more self-confident for this interaction."

I heard a sigh of relief on the phone. "Yes, I can already feel how this makes it much easier for me."

19

IT'S EASIER TO FEEL SELF-CONFIDENT WHEN YOU ARE IN A POSITIVE STATE OF MIND

Your state of mind impacts your self-confidence. When you are feeling joyful or happy, you are more optimistic and feel better about yourself. In a good state of mind, your self-confidence will rise.

If you are ever in a negative emotional state, you are likely to feel less self-confident. It's not that you suddenly became less knowledgeable, less skilled and talented, or less competent. Rather, when you are in a high mood your focus is much more positive than when you are in a low mood.

Shlomo Hamelech (King Solomon) provides a formula for feeling good and for the opposite. The verse (*Mishlei* 15:15) states: "All the days of the poor are bad. But for a person with a good mind, life is likened to constant parties." The Hebrew wording of the second half of this verse is *"tov leiv, mishteh tamid."* Rabbi Avigdor Miller always translated *"tov leiv"* as a person with a "good mind." He elaborated that the word *leiv*, which literally means *heart*, is referring to the *mind*. And that is why he translated *Chovos Halevavos* — which is often translated as "Duties of the Hearts" — as, "Duties of the Mind." The classic work deals with the vital importance of our thoughts. Spiritual thoughts connect us with the Creator, enabling us to experience much gratitude and love for Hashem.

People who have mastered happiness and joy personify this lesson. We are constantly breathing and we should be grateful for each and every breath. As long as we are alive, we have an opportunity to be joyful for being alive. Everyone can learn to do this more frequently. It takes practice. And with the focus of our minds on the great experience of being alive, being joyful can become a wonderful habit. I have elaborated on this theme in *Gateway to Happiness,* which was published in 1983.

Just reading a book about happiness doesn't guarantee happiness, however. Only your thoughts and your mind can create happiness for you. Realizing this, you will be more motivated to make it a habit to be more grateful and more appreciate of all the gifts the Creator has bestowed upon you in the past and continues bestowing in the present.

It has been shown that we must practice any skill or talent for 10,000 hours to gain expertise. I don't know anyone who has practiced being grateful and appreciative for all the Almighty's gifts for 10,000 hours and has not mastered this way of being. Most people who haven't mastered happiness didn't spend 10,000 hours practicing before deciding that it's too hard for them to be happy.

But even someone who is not yet an expert at happiness and joy can still choose to think the thoughts necessary for happiness. Even someone who is not an expert can speak and act in ways that are conducive to happiness and joy.

While one does not need to be happy to experience self-confidence, it helps. It's so much easier for a master of happiness and joy to be self-confident.

In addition to thinking appreciatively and gratefully, there are other healthy ways of getting into a positive state of mind. The acronym is LSD. These letters often refer to an illegal, mood-changing chemical. But they also refer to positive, mind-altering behaviors: Laughing, Singing, and Dancing. When you laugh, your brain produces a healthy chemical that puts you in a better state of mind. When you sing a joyful tune and dance accordingly, your brain produces the chemicals that put you into a positive state of mind.

It has been said we should be grateful for being in a positive state of mind and graceful when we are in a low state of mind. As you train your mind to think in better ways and you speak and act accordingly, you will find that it's easier for you to have a higher level of self-confidence.

Every moment of happiness and joy is added to your mental library. The more you feel this way, the more it becomes part of your regular way of being. Knowing that you will be able to make this your habitual pattern should give you self-confidence, even if you are not yet able to be happy and joyful as often as you would like. Enjoy the process. The more optimistic you are about your success at this, the faster you will get there. You are always in the right time and place to improve yourself.

Someone who was in a very low mood said to me, "The reason I am in such a low mood is because I lack self-confidence. If only I were more self-confident, than I would feel happier."

"There is some truth in what you say," I agreed. "But it's a lot easier to feel self-confident when you are in a positive emotional state of mind. Let's review your thoughts when you were in your best emotional states. What are you grateful for? What have been your greatest moments of joy? How can you use your imagination to imagine great things happening?"

As we talked, his mood lifted and his feelings of self-confidence returned.

20
MAINTAINING SELF-CONFIDENCE
WHEN CHALLENGED BY PESSIMISTS

Even the most talented and capable people will be challenged by pessimists. These are people who focus on negative possibilities. They might have tried things themselves that didn't work out, or know a lot of people who were not successful. If you are self-confident, they will tell you why your self-confidence is not warranted. Don't automatically assume that others are correct when they try to dissuade you.

Even though self-confidence is an inside quality, it is understandable that challenges from people who don't see your potential might shake that confidence. Some might be well meaning and are trying to "protect you from being disappointed." Others are just generally skeptical until proven wrong.

We need to be open to objective feedback. Perhaps the questions about our abilities or qualifications are valid. On the other hand, the other person's negativity might not reflect our actual abilities and potential. Perhaps it just reflects his own self-image. When you have realistic self-confidence, you have a better chance of success.

Many experts were pessimistic about major accomplishments being reached, yet they were achieved by people with self-confidence in their goals. Many people with remarkable talent weren't recognized as talented by everyone they met, but eventually it became obvious to all that these self-confident people really had the talent they thought they had.

When you have a strong sense of self-confidence in what you wish to do, don't allow unwarranted negativity to stop you. In many situations, it is better to have tried, even if things don't work as planned. When you don't try, you are 100 percent guaranteed that you won't accomplish and you won't succeed. Even if the chances of success don't seem that strong right now, you can't be certain that things won't work out.

Only by trying do we gain more knowledge of what we can and can't do at this time. When the benefits are high, it is often worth taking the risk. If you have pure motives for what you are trying to do, it was wise to try.

Taking action in the face of pessimism builds your self-confidence. Even if you only achieve and accomplish on a much smaller scale than planned, your accomplishment shows you that you can really do more than the naysayers thought.

Some people with high levels of self-confidence had to try again and again before they succeeded. Their confident attitude enabled them to keep trying when others with less self-confidence would have given up. They were patient and persisted. Their persistence paid off big dividends.

We have lightbulbs because Edison viewed the first 10,000 tries as just experiments showing what wouldn't work. We have telephones today because Alexander Graham Bell wasn't stopped by those who thought he was just a dreamer. We have airplanes because the Wright brother kept on keeping on. There are radios and other forms of wireless communication because Marconi refused to be stopped.

The greatest people became great because they weren't stopped by people who did not share their vision. Don't let a lack of self-confidence stop you from doing all you can to succeed. Don't allow pessimists to diminish your self-confidence. Many times in life people have had to make many attempts before they accomplished what they had hoped to accomplish. The deep conviction that they would reach their goal led to tremendous success.

I had the merit of watching Rabbi Noah Weinberg firsthand for many years. He had tremendous goals. But there were many people who thought that his goals were totally unrealistic. His motto was to cite the aphorism, "Winners never quit; and quitters never win." He faced adversity with a tremendous inner spirit. He knew that what he had set out to do could be accomplished. Today the two gigantic buildings of Aish Hatorah opposite the Western Wall are a testimony to his indomitable spirit.

21
SELF-CONFIDENT ROLE MODELS

Flip through the pages of history to find real-life role models of self-confidence. Some people with great self-confidence were brilliant. They were creative geniuses. They had phenomenal memories.

It's easy to say, "Of course that person had self-confidence. If I were blessed with a mind like his, I too would be very self-confident."

Many role models of self-confident success weren't born with unusual talents. They became skilled by practicing over and over again. They became knowledgeable by studying and reviewing what they learned.

A tremendous number of people were not brilliant scholars, but they applied themselves. They studied diligently. They found teachers and mentors. They reviewed, over and over again. They didn't give up. And their inner drive enabled them to persevere and accomplish what might have seemed impossible.

You too can create that inner drive. You too can patiently review ideas over and over again. You too can try repeatedly and gain from trial and error. You can learn what you are doing right. And you learn from mistakes to see what needs to be improved.

Little children are the best role models for self-confident persistence. Watch a little boy or girl learning to crawl. They don't give up. They have an inner drive and they aren't stopped by obstacles. They get tired of crawling. They rest. And they try again. Then they learn to stand up and walk. They fall down. But they self-confidently pick themselves up. They begin to talk. They don't always pronounce words correctly, so their parents and older siblings correct them. Eventually they learn to speak fluently. This process is true for every single person who can presently walk and talk.

The problem for most people is not that they didn't have the innate talent. Instead, they didn't practice enough. They didn't review, and they gave up too soon. They didn't do what role models of success in all different areas have done. And therefore they lack self-confidence.

Lack of self-confidence is not really what is holding you back. Lack of practice prevents you from being able to say and do what you need to say and do. Then you can easily talk yourself into believing that it's a lack of self-confidence, not lack of practice, that is holding you back. You also need teachers, mentors, or coaches to teach you what you need to do to be more successful.

When you see a potential role model, try to find out more information about how he became the type of person you want to emulate. You might be able to speak to the person himself. You might be able to speak to people who knew him. You might read articles and books that he studied or even books that he wrote. You might read his biography. You might read the books and biographies that influenced and inspired that person.

If you cannot personally interview a role model, try to imagine that you have an opportunity to interview that person. Using your imagination, ask questions about his self-confidence. Ask him what attitudes enabled him to do what he did.

Then be patient. When you are in a very calm state of mind, wait for answers. Your mind will create answers. Pretending to interview that real person is a tool for your own mind to creatively build your own self-confidence.

If you think that you are not creative enough to imagine an interview with your role model, you have creatively created an imaginary limitation for yourself. Every human being has a creative potential, but not everyone recognizes their own creativity. In *Building Your Self-image* I described how a conversation with the late Rabbi Avraham Pincus (father of Rav Shimshon Pincus) in 1980 got me to recognize my own creativity. I had already been creative but didn't recognize it as such. He pointed it out to me. Since then I have the awareness that we all are creative.

One of the most self-confident public speakers I know told me that when he was growing up he considered himself to be of just mediocre intelligence. He had some brilliant relatives who were child prodigies, and he compared himself to them. His unique style of brilliance was only manifest in later years.

After much experience, I have learned that although some people are self-confident at a young age, many others only develop their self-confidence later on in life.

22

WAKE UP TO YOUR INNER GREATNESS

My father's teacher, Rabbi Yosef Kahaneman of Ponevez, used to say to students, "Imagine that you had a dream in which you were being chased by lions, tigers, and bears. You felt a desperate need to escape, but any direction you turned to, you saw these wild animals approaching. You feel terrified and desperate. What could you do to save yourself?"

He answered gently, "Wake up! When you wake up, you realize that all the fear and terror were produced by your imagination. It was all in your own mind. You are actually safe. There weren't any actual lions, tigers, or bears. All is well."

Similarly, you can wake up to your inner greatness and choose great words and actions.

We can easily imagine all kinds of misfortunes, disasters, and catastrophes. Most people are prisoners of limiting and counterproductive thoughts and beliefs. All we need to do is wake up to the great opportunities that the Creator keeps giving us. When we wake up, we realize that we are much more capable than we previously thought. When we utilize our real abilities and potential to the fullest, we can create great things for ourselves and for others.

We have had the potential for authentic inner greatness since birth. Greatness is not about fame and glory or an outward appearance of success. It is about connecting with our Creator and doing His will with joy and love. It is about choosing more elevated thoughts, words, and actions, moment by moment and day by day. It is about handling challenges and adversity with wise, clear thinking and inner courage. It is about living up to great ideals even when it might be difficult to do so. It is about being resilient and bouncing back when faced with mistakes, setbacks, and disappointments.

The foundation for a life of authentic greatness includes an awareness of the greatness of our eternal soul and our connection with the Creator and Sustainer of the universe. Living with this awareness elevates us.

The greatest spiritual giants of all the generations have taught that this inner greatness is the Divine Soul within you. It influences your thoughts, words, and actions. Your relationship with your Self is on a higher plane.

The emotional life of a person with elevated Torah greatness is infused with a *simchah* and *ahavah* of *kedushah* (holy joy and love). The foundation of this path is an ongoing state of basic well-being and inner peace. Your *middos* (character traits) reflect an inner dignity and you interact with others in exemplary ways. Your Torah study, prayers, and words and acts of kindness are infused with a holiness that is infinite and eternal.

This book is not only for the select few of the greatest people who are always aware of their inner greatness. It is for individuals like me, people who experience many ups and downs. Don't read it with the concern and worry that we are not always in touch with our inner greatness. This book was written to encourage myself and to share these thoughts so others may gain from them. We lived with a limited view of who we are and what we can do and accomplish. This book should upgrade our consciousness of our inner greatness.

Becoming aware of how we think, speak, and act in our various states helps us better balance our ups and downs. When we are up, we are on a much higher spiritual place than when we are down. Our task is to identify how we behave when we are up. Having this "up" self-image will make it easier for us to gracefully face the "downs" in an upward direction.

You are unique and your greatness is unique to you. As discussed in *Life Is Now* (ArtScroll, 2009), you are always in the present. Even when reviewing your memories of the past or thinking about plans for the future, you are always in the present moment. And in any present moment you have free will to choose great thoughts, great words, and great actions.

On *Yom Kippur*, we experience a heightened spirituality. This feeling can influence the way we act the entire year. Moments of awareness of our inner greatness can influence us throughout the day and throughout our lives.

When Adam, the first man, was first created, he had unparalleled greatness and was given a world to appreciate. The Torah gives Noah the title of a *tzadik tamim*, a totally righteous person.

He found favor (*chein*) in the eyes of Hashem. We are all descendants of Adam and Noah. As we reveal the inner greatness that we inherited from them, we will be motivated to live on a higher plane and be a more positive influence on the lives of those we encounter.

Let the ideas in this book permeate your consciousness for a few moments. Later on, let these ideas influence your thoughts. And when you speak and act you might find that these words and ideas have inspired you to choose elevated thoughts and actions. When you need an emotional or spiritual boost, let your moments of inspiration serve as a shining light to make it easier to see your way upward and forward.

I have a photograph of me saying my bar-mitzvah speech to the Ponevezer Rav with my father listening in the background. My bar mitzvah was many years ago.

Ever since I heard the "wake up from your dream" idea in the name of Rabbi Yosef Kahaneman, this picture reminds me that we all need to wake up to our inner greatness.

In addition, if you are confident about someone else's inner greatness, you can even inspire him to strive for more.

23
HIGHLIGHT SELF-CONFIDENCE

Each day has its highlights. At the end of the day, think about the moments when you felt, spoke, and acted at your happiest and most joyful of the day to find the highlights of happiness and joy. You have kindness highlights in the moments when you spoke and acted with kindness, or when someone else spoke and acted with kindness toward you. These moments serve as lessons for you to also speak and act with similar kindness.

Each day you also have your self-confidence highlights, found in the moments when you were most self-confident. These highlights can be words or actions that express authentic self-confidence.

If you didn't speak or act with self-confidence in a given day, that night you can imagine yourself speaking and acting with self-confidence. Using your imagination is a powerful tool to condition your mind to be more self-confident.

Just as each day has its highlights, so too each week, month, and year has its highlights. You can review your weekly highlights every week and your monthly accomplishments every month. On your birthday you can review your year's highlights that show you at your most self-confident. The more conscious you are about those highlights, the greater the impact they will have on your life.

And the ultimate in your personal highlights are the lifetime highlights, when you spoke and acted with the greatest self-confidence. You are not in a contest with anyone else. This is not a sporting event where the goal is to do better than someone else. This is awareness of a personal achievement. Regardless of another person's self-confidence, your own self-confidence is what matters in your life. By all means, learn from others to keep increasing your own self-confidence. But if something is challenging for you to say and do, you need self-confidence to say and do it.

A key benefit of focusing on your own self-confidence highlights is that it removes your focus from your limitations. People who keep complaining, "I'm not as self-confident as I would like to be," become experts on lacking self-confidence. That is not the path to reach high levels of self-confidence. The way to increase your self-confidence is to keep your mental focus on what you have already said and done that is an expression of self-confidence. Then you will notice even higher and greater self-confidence.

The very fact that you are reading this section means that you are presently thinking about self-confidence highlights. So you can say to yourself, *Thinking right now about my self-confident highlights is a self-confident highlight for today.*

You might think of two or three self-confident highlights one day. You might think of five self-confident highlights or even ten self-confident highlights. The number isn't that important. It's the focus that makes a difference.

Someone who heard that I was writing a book on self-confidence said to me, "I wish I could be more self-confident. But when I think of the subject of self-confidence, I recall many times and moments when I wasn't self-confident. I feel bad just hearing the words 'self-confidence.'"

"There are many other people in the same boat," I said to him. "One of the easiest remedies in this situation is to collect self-confident highlights. Even if you feel you lack self-confidence, I'm certain that sometimes you feel greater self-confidence than at other times. From now on, let the word 'self-confidence' serve as a reminder of your self-confident highlights."

He agreed that this was a great idea and reported back that it worked for him. Let's see if this will work for you.

24

THE SELF-CONFIDENT PART OF YOU

People often use the expression of "parts" as in, "Part of me felt comfortable about doing it and part of me felt uncomfortable." Or, "Part of me wanted to do it, but another part felt it would be impossible to do." In reality we have one soul, one brain, one mind. But since this expression is used, it can be utilized to create a "self-confident part."

Even if you think and feel that you lack self-confidence, you can still create a self-confident part. The self-confident part of you can say and do things you can't yet do. It's almost as if "you" are not saying or doing them; your "part" is.

Not everyone relates to this idea. If you can access your self-confident state at will, there is no real need to imagine a self-confident part. But if you find it challenging to access self-confidence, creating a self-confident part can make it much easier for you to actually speak and act with self-confidence.

So if you ever catch yourself thinking, *I lack the self-confidence to say or do that*, hear an inner voice telling you, *You don't have to say or do that. Your self-confident part will take over and joyfully speak and act with self-confidence.*

My experience has shown that people who do this a number of times eventually realize that they can accomplish what they initially thought they couldn't. Only their subjective thoughts had limited them, and now they stopped needlessly limiting themselves.

Many people would love to be able to raise funds for worthy causes. They are idealistic and know that the cause they want to help sponsor is very worthwhile. But they say they are not a fund-raiser and they can't do it. When they change their self-talk to the self-talk of a confident fund-raiser who can ask anyone for anything, they will be able to do it. Letting their self-confident part ask for them is a tool that will make it easier when they first start. This could make the entire process enjoyable and easy. This creates a breakthrough that will benefit all those who gain from that funding.

What positive actions do you find difficult? Let your self-confident part say and do those things. Once it does, you have this experience in your life history forever, and you can access it whenever you need a burst of self-confidence.

Someone who wanted to teach young children told me about the challenge he faced.

"I love teaching young children and I feel very self-confident that I can do a wonderful job. I know I will be a great teacher. But I get intimidated and flustered when being interviewed by those who will

hire me. What can I do to present myself as the self-confident teacher I know I am?"

"Once you are hired, I'm certain you will do an excellent job," I reassured him. I explained the idea of creating a self-confident part to interact with interviewers.

"Just let your self-confident part handle the interview for you!"

He did and it worked out well for everyone.

25

CHOICES AFTER
A ROUGH CHILDHOOD

"It's understandable why I lack self-confidence," some people say. "It's because of my childhood."

Many people believe that a rough childhood creates a problematic life. But in reality, one's current choice of thoughts, words, and actions determines one's emotional states in the present. Regardless of one's childhood, if a person consistently thinks, speaks, and acts with self-confidence in the present, he will be a self-confident person. Not only will he think, speak, and act with self-confidence, he will also feel self-confident.

A person's feelings are based on what is going on in his mind in the present moment. Take laughter. If someone finds something funny and laughs in any present moment, his laughter will put him in a better state. When a person laughs it doesn't matter what his childhood has been like; laughter puts his entire physical system into a complex reaction that has many health benefits.

His breathing, brain waves, blood pressure, energy level, heartbeat, hormones, immune system, muscle tension, posture, facial expression, and tone of voice will all be consistent with the beneficial states that automatically occur when he accesses the pleasurable state called "laughter."

It doesn't matter how his parents treated him in the past or what his early or later environment was like; it doesn't matter what his teachers, employers, friends, relatives, and neighbors thought of him. When he laughs at something he finds funny, he feels good.

What happens to anyone in a laughing state is similar to that what happens when someone is in a self-confident state. At that moment, his entire mind and body is in this state. Our states depend on what we are thinking, saying, and doing right now in the present.

It's much easier to be self-confident if one had great genes, great parents, great teachers, great friends, and a great environment growing up. But just as laughing in the present is a present reality regardless of the past, so too a present moment of total self-confidence is a great state, regardless of what happened before.

Many people claim that the past causes the future, and there is truth to that. Our past influences our present. But a moment of laughter in the present works the same, regardless of the past. So, too, a moment of self-confidence in the present works to influence our thoughts, feelings, words, and actions, regardless of the past.

We can't undo what already happened. But we can choose our next thoughts, our next words, and our next actions. Right now and for the rest of your life, you can choose to think, speak, and act with great self-confidence just because you choose to think, speak, and act this way. Although you have the ability to claim that you can't because of various occurrences of the past, it's not really your childhood and past that are holding you back. Only your thoughts about your right and ability to have self-confidence are limiting your confidence.

Some of the greatest achievers and accomplishers in the world have been people with awful childhoods and awful pasts. But they didn't let the past stop them from accomplishing and achieving. You, too, can choose to claim your right to live a life of self-confidence. This is 100 percent dependent upon your present attitude. You have the same right to have the self-confidence as the most self-confident people who have ever lived. Have the self-confidence to achieve and accomplish whatever is humanly possible for you to accomplish.

Someone who had been in therapy for a long time attended a class I gave on building self-image and self-confidence.

He argued vehemently that if someone grew up in a very deprived early environment, he can't be expected to be the same as someone who grew up in an emotionally enriched environment.

"I agree with you," I responded. "A positive early environment is a big plus in a person's life. We can't change the past. Everything that we already experienced, we already experienced. But our perspective about our past is how that past will affect us in the present and future. I've seen time and again that those who made it a habit to blame their past created barriers and blocks for themselves. On the other hand, people who took 100 percent responsibility for creating a great life were able to overcome major handicaps.

"Determination and intensity of will to succeed have changed people's lives. When you intensify your will to live a meaningful, self-confident life, you will eventually be able to create an inner happiness that will be with you for the rest of your life. The human mind and soul has the ability to do this. I wish you success in creating a great life for yourself."

26
TAKE A SELF-CONFIDENCE WALK

Walk each day. Walk for greater health. Walk for greater clarity of mind. When you walk, your mental state becomes calmer. When you walk you have a wonderful opportunity to think of ways to improve your character and your life. Whenever you want to increase your self-confidence, take a self-confidence walk.

You can reflect on this book's ideas for building self-confidence when you take a self-confidence walk. Even if this is the only chapter you read, you now know that people who take self-confidence walks can build their self-confidence just by walking.

Whatever you think in a given moment has a direct impact on your feelings at that moment. So if you take a self-confidence walk when you need a boost of self-confidence, your positive thoughts during that walk will increase your feelings of self-confidence at that time.

Success with this technique depends on the wording of the person who takes the self-confidence walk. To ensure it *doesn't* work, be upset that you don't have as much self-confidence as you would wish, think about how awful it is that you need to walk to increase your self-confidence, and compare yourself negatively to people with more self-confidence. Repeat negative statements to feel worse and lower your self-confidence. People who are aware of the power of their thinking will be wise not to think this way.

Since you are the type of person who appreciates self-confidence, you want to do positive things to increase feelings of self-confidence. So when you take your self-confidence-building walks, think about how wonderful it is that you are alive and that you can walk. Be grateful for the many things that you have been grateful for already and add new reasons to be grateful. With these good feelings, think about how you will benefit from more self-confidence.

Walking helps your mind be more creative. So a self-confident walk will be beneficial for creatively thinking of what you will be able to do with your increased self-confidence.

Smile while you take your self-confident walk. Smiling will make it easier to greet other people with a smile to boost their spirits. And your own inner state will be raised, regardless of the state you were in when you began your self-confident walk.

A world-famous performer known for his powerful impact on large crowds had a secret: Even after many years of performing, he felt insecure before each performance. Right before he appeared on stage, he would walk a considerable distance while mentally building up his courage and self-confidence. It worked for him, and it can work for you.

27

THE CLASSIC "IF YOU KNEW YOU COULDN'T FAIL" QUESTION

There is another classic question in coaching circles: "If you knew you couldn't fail, what goal or dream would you strive for?" This is also sometimes worded as, "If you were guaranteed success, what goal or dream would you strive for?"

People have goals or dreams that they would love to achieve, but the fear of failure prevents them from taking action. Some people are more afraid that their goal or dream is impossible. Although some things are humanly impossible, many things are possible and were already accomplished by other people. But many times when people feel that they don't have the skills, talents, resources, intelligence, or time to accomplish, or are missing another factor, they don't even try to reach for their dreams.

When these people build their self-confidence, the "impossible" becomes "worth a try." Self-confidence doesn't guarantee success. But not trying guarantees no success.

Some people could use a mentor or coach to boost their motivation and point out helpful ideas that they might not have thought of on their own. With added self-confidence, even without any input from anyone else, people are more likely to see possibilities that weren't visible before.

Your mind is capable of magnificent things. Self-confidence enables you to utilize your intelligence, imagination, and creativity that are hidden without self-confidence. People with self-confidence speak and act in ways that express more inner talent and intelligence. Self-confidence ignites abilities, skills, and talents.

When you have self-confidence you are not afraid of trying and failing. You view trying as an experiment. And experiments never fail: They show whether or not you can do something in a certain way. You learn from each experiment to grow closer to reaching your goals and dreams.

Use your imagination to imagine yourself having a high dose of self-confidence. Then say, *I am so extremely self-confident that even if my experiment doesn't work out as well as I was hoping, I will still be in a state of well-being. What could I say or do to further my journey toward my goals and dreams?*

Someone who had a history of quitting shared with me, "I finally decided to quit quitting when I realized that persistence is the number-one quality I needed to develop."

He continued, "I envied individuals who would continue trying long after I had already given up and quit. But then I was told that anyone can become a person who persists. Giving up is a habit. And persisting is a habit. Like everyone else with any positive habit, I can begin to develop persistence at any time.

"I began to realize that when I was a young child, I persisted when I enjoyed what I was doing. I recalled more times when I quit as I got older and didn't persist as long as I should have. But my memories of persisting as a child were still there in my mental library.

"I eventually realized that the only reason I tended to quit was because I had told myself, 'What's the use of continuing to try, when I know I'll fail?' But I made up my mind not to say this to myself any more if I couldn't be absolutely certain that I would fail.

"Before, my attitude was that unless I was certain to succeed, I would give up. Now I turned it around. As long as I wasn't certain that I would fail, I was going to persist. I knew that I could never really be certain I would fail. This has made a major impact on my life."

28

USE MIRRORS TO BUILD YOUR SELF-CONFIDENCE

When you talk to yourself while looking in a mirror, your words have a stronger impact than when you merely think a specific thought. It's almost as if you are talking to someone else and listening to what that person says.

You can use this power to condition your mind in ways that create better ways of being. This is true for all the positive traits and qualities that you would like to integrate. Since your current intention is to increase your self-confidence, mirrors can be used as a tool to increase your conscious self-confidence. You can choose to use the next three mirrors, or the next ten mirrors, or all the mirrors you see for a week. You decide.

When you see yourself in a mirror, say enthusiastically (or quietly, if more appropriate), *Right now and forever, I choose to think, speak, and act with greater and greater self-confidence.*

Repeating this message enough times will help you internalize and integrate it. This works amazingly well for some people. Only your own experiences will be able to determine how it works for you. But if you are sincere about this working for you, be persistent. Every repetition deepens and strengthens your self-confidence.

A word of warning: If you want to prove that this suggestion won't work, your mind will make certain that you are right. But if you allow yourself to be objective about testing it out and really want it to work for you, it might work. And if you believe wholeheartedly that this will work for you, it will increase your self-confidence.

If someone argues, "This won't work for anyone," I reply that I know with 100 percent certainty that this does work for some people.

Someone I knew well was going through a very challenging time. The moodiness it created caused him to lose touch with his inner self-confidence. He felt awful about not being as happy as he knew he could be.

"What can I do to regain my self-confidence?" he asked.

When I suggested he serve as his own self-confidence coach by encouraging himself as he looked in a mirror, he said to me, "But I don't feel comfortable about doing that."

"You're not alone," I said to him. "But do it anyway. Keep it up. Mirrors used wisely make a powerful impact. If you tell yourself, 'This is silly. I resent the idea that I need to do this ridiculous exercise. I shouldn't have to do this,' then you will feel uncomfortable. It's not the mirror that's causing these feelings. It's your thoughts and self-talk that creates them.

"You can choose to tell yourself, 'I'm grateful that I can see myself in the mirror and that I know how to condition my mind in positive

ways. This has worked for others and it will work for me. It's very intelligent to know how to condition my mind. Every time I practice this I will feel better and better as my self-confidence gets stronger and stronger.'"

He no longer considers this silly!

29

A COMMON MISTAKE ABOUT SELF-CONFIDENCE

Many people mistakenly think that an air of superiority reveals self-confidence. People with this attitude always assume they are right and others are wrong. They might feel positive about themselves, but they lack an accurate perspective. They could be blind to their own faults and mistakes. Others can easily feel uncomfortable in their presence.

True self-confidence is an inner recognition of the tremendous value of each and every human being. Therefore, one feels an unconditionally positive attitude about one's own essence and applies this recognition to all other people also. We are all part of the Almighty's creation and contain a spark of Divinity.

Kind, compassionate truth-seekers prioritize, making each person they encounter feel special. They have no need to show off or to boast. They don't try to make other feel inferior. They are truly elevated and have no need for artificial means of self-aggrandizement.

Many people who are honest about their own self-confidence and personal deficiencies might be intimidated by those who try to hide their limitations and frailties. These honest people might think less of themselves because they unnecessarily compare themselves with others who project higher levels of self-confidence.

As a general rule: If you feel that someone is purposely trying to intimidate you, that alone is a valid reason not to allow yourself to be intimidated. He is trying to inflate himself at your expense. See through his mask. It's just like a costume in a play. It isn't real.

"When I was younger, I was fooled by arrogant and conceited people into thinking that I was worth less than them," someone confided in me. "My parents were sincere about who they were. They never did things just for outward appearances. I felt inferior. I wished my family and I were more self-confident.

"But as I grew up, my eyes were opened. I realized that I was taken in by actors. Sincerity and authenticity are more valuable than counterfeit and superficial shows of confidence. Many of those people had an inner emptiness that they tried to cover up and hide.

"I am no longer in a contest with anyone else. It is not for me to judge who is real and who isn't. My mission in life is to be the best me that I can be. And I have sufficient self-confidence to strive for that."

30
BEING PROPERLY PREPARED
HELPS YOUR SELF-CONFIDENCE

When you are properly prepared, it is easier to be self-confident. This is true whether it's for a talk or class you have to give, a meeting you have to attend, or a sales presentation you have to present.

When you have to give a talk or a class, regardless of how self-confident you are about yourself, you have to know certain information. The better you know that information, the more comfortable you will feel.

People who are afraid to make mistakes or not knowing the answer will feel more stress than someone who is not afraid. There are two methods for letting go of such a fear. One way is to be very well prepared. When you prepare well, you are confident that you know what you need to know. The other way is to feel a strong sense of your own value and worth at all times. Although you don't want to make mistakes, you know your value as a person is not dependent on perfection and you calmly accept any mistakes. This is not an "I-don't-care" attitude; it is a wise balance of wanting to do as well as you can, and a modest acceptance of the fact that you are a fallible human being.

Some people are overly perfectionistic. They are extremely afraid of making trivial mistakes. They are very nervous about having to say, "I don't know." This fear is a bad habit. Wanting to do well is a valid human need. Not wanting to make mistakes even when a mistake will not have consequences can be an admirable quality. It is the exaggerated fear that is a problem.

Inner calm and serenity are conducive to physical and mental health. Small amounts of stress can be beneficial. But excessive stress in situations that are not life threatening comes from thoughts that are not based on the situation. Healthier and wiser thoughts can free you from these unnecessary feelings.

Allow yourself to be calm about preparing for what you need to know. Someone who looks at a mistake or a lack of knowledge as an extreme problem is likely to be nervous. The more self-confidence you build up, the more calm you will be about preparing. You are doing all that you can possibly do.

Once you have internalized and integrated the attitudes necessary for self-confidence, even if you aren't properly prepared you can still experience self-confidence. You might not know everything you wanted to know, but your general feeling is a self-confident one. You know that you are able to handle situations well. You know that you can ask questions and learn more. You know what you know and you know what you still need to learn. You feel good about your essential self, regardless of how well you do.

To summarize: To be self-confident when presenting information to others, prepare what you can. Have a wise and calm attitude about the results. Being calm will help you prepare and remember at higher levels of efficiency.

A very successful lecturer shared with me, "When I began teaching, I was extremely nervous about making even very minor mistakes. If I realized I had erred in some trivial way, I would obsess over the mistake. This created a great deal of stress in my life.

"An older, more established person once heard a talk that I gave. He told me afterward that he liked what he heard. He had heard me before, and he commented on my progress.

"Then he told me, 'I noticed how frustrated you became when someone corrected a minor point. I too used to feel awful about making mistakes. But as I got older I realized that it's normal to make mistakes. A person of character acknowledges them. With age I gained a greater perspective of how important something really is in the scheme of things. I learned to differentiate between what will really make a difference and what won't. I learned to just let it go. I didn't waste time and energy on past mistakes. My focus was on the good that I can accomplish in the present and in the future. Now I suggest to younger people: Feel a sense of accomplishment with the good you are doing. And make it your goal to constantly improve as you keep accomplishing more and more.'"

This person learned a lesson we all need. Prepare as well as you can, but don't exaggerate the significance of an imperfection. Absolute perfection is only the Almighty's. Be wise. Be humble. And do as well as you can in any situation, with a sense of gratitude for the gifts the Almighty has given you.

31

FEELING COMFORTABLE WHEN YOU MEET NEW PEOPLE

Self-confidence helps you feel more comfortable when you meet new people. Self-consciousness makes a person feel uncomfortable in those same situations. What is the difference? Your thoughts.

Self-consciousness comes from an excessive fear of being judged negatively. Self-consciousness is created by thoughts such as, *I hope I don't make a bad impression on this person. I hope this person will like me. I hope this person won't be judgmental and critical of me. I hope that I don't make a fool of myself.*

It's natural to want to make a good impression. The more comfortable you are about yourself, the less nervous you will be about what other people think of you.

People concerned about kindness are more conscious about what they can do for others than about what others are thinking about them. They want to be of service to others. They want to make others feel good. They want to help others in any way that they can. Since their focus is on the other person, they are free from the concern about the judgment of others.

Self-confidence includes the attitude, *Of course, I would like others to like me and feel good about me. But that's secondary to my concern about what I can do to be kind to others.*

Thoughts of self-confident people center around, *What can I do to help you?* Therefore they are free from thinking, *How are you judging me?*

When people are kind and sincerely like other people, the vast majority of other people feel positive about them. They gain the esteem of others. They don't need to focus on creating this response. It will be an automatic outcome of their positive regard for themselves and their sincere wish to speak and act kindly.

The ironic thing is: The less you try to make a good impression while being an authentically kind person, the better impression you automatically make.

We all need oxygen for our survival. When you are in a situation when oxygen is plentiful and your lungs are working properly, you don't need to focus on getting oxygen. You automatically keep breathing and inhaling all the necessary oxygen. You are not conscious of the act of breathing. This is the attitude of someone who has strong self-respect and respect for others: He gains respect, but isn't conscious about actively achieving it.

In order to feel comfortable when you meet new people, become comfortable about yourself. This is also known as self-confidence. People will feel good in your presence and you don't need to make a conscious effort to impress them.

Someone with a reputation of being a gregarious extrovert who positively influenced many people shared with me, "I used to be very self-conscious when meeting someone I didn't know. Eventually I realized that my discomfort was based on my concern about what others were thinking of me. But the reality is that most people were much more concerned about what I was thinking of them. Moreover, even if someone was thinking something negative about me, it usually didn't make any practical difference in my life. People think many thousands of thoughts a day with the positive and negative thoughts interspersed throughout. Much of what a person thinks about isn't consciously remembered for very long.

"This awareness freed me. I now consider meeting new people as one of my greatest pleasures in life. Is this self-confidence? I guess it is."

32
WITHOUT SELF-CONFIDENCE, YOU DON'T USE YOUR TOTAL POTENTIAL

We all have our inner strengths and limitations. With self-confidence, we empower more of our inner strengths. Without self-confidence, we empower our limitations.

Self-confidence is not a guarantee. Even with self-confidence, you might not be successful. You might do worse than you thought. You might not say what needs to be said and might not do what needs to be done. On the other hand, even without self-confidence, you might be successful. You might do better than you thought. You might say and do what needs to be said and done.

But it is more likely that with self-confidence you will do better than without self-confidence. Lack of self-confidence will prevent you from being all that you could have been.

It doesn't cost money to have self-confidence. It doesn't take much time to have self-confidence. And it doesn't use a lot of energy to have self-confidence.

You create your self-confidence with your attitude and mindset toward yourself. Some people naturally have more self-confidence, and some people need to make an effort to acquire it. But since self-confidence is a mental quality, you can decide to create and access this way of thinking and feeling.

The more frequently you practice being self-confident, the more automatically you will act that way. Even someone who didn't have self-confidence can wisely decide, *I am going to create all the self-confidence that I can.*

Only your own thoughts about self-confidence can stop you from having self-confidence. Truly self-confident people make their self-confidence independent of whether others believe in them or not. They make their present self-confidence independent of past successes and failures. They know that at any given moment they can choose to think, feel, speak, and act with self-confidence.

In life we have much potential. Self-confidence enables us to utilize more potential. We all have much potential self-confidence. Claiming it and choosing to benefit from it turns that potential into reality.

All over our planet there are people who fail to apply what they know. You will come across them wherever you go. Although they could be extremely successful and create very happy lives with their intelligence and knowledge, they aren't. They needlessly limit themselves with their lack of self-confidence.

From very accomplished people we learn the extent of what human beings are capable of achieving. Even very simple people have reached higher levels of achievement because of their self-confidence.

Be compassionate when you encounter people who failed to utilize their potential, but learn from them the harm caused by a lack of self-confidence. Commit yourself to continue developing your own self-confidence.

I once envisioned a club with too many members. The name of the club is, "Those who failed to accomplish as much as they really could." To become a member of the more advanced club, "Those who are in the process of doing, being, and accomplishing more than before club," improve your self-confidence.

33

SELF-CONFIDENT BREATHING

When you take in oxygen with each breath, also inhale self-confidence. You breathe from the time you wake up in the morning until you go to sleep at night. Actually, you even breathe in your sleep! Utilize your breath to breathe in self-confidence.

Try out this sentence: "With each and every breath, I am becoming more and more self-confident."

Now repeat this sentence: "With each and every breath, I am becoming more and more self-confident."

And now repeat this a third time: "With each and every breath, I am becoming more and more self-confident."

This is easy to say, isn't it?

Every time you repeat this simple sentence you associate breathing with inhaling self-confidence. After enough repetitions, your brain uses this tool to automatically connect breathing and increasing your self-confidence. You breathe without thinking about it; this repetition helps you be self-confident without thought, too.

Those who are confident that it will eventually work have found that this does work after repeated repetitions. But if someone wants to prove that he won't be able to breathe in self-confidence, it won't work for him. All he needs to say is, "I might repeat that with each breath I am becoming more and more self-confident, but this won't work for me."

Your belief about whether you can increase your self-confidence by breathing is a key factor in whether or not it will be effective. Believe it won't work and it won't. Believe it will work and it will.

As a self-confident coach, I want you to be successful at increasing your self-confidence. So I highly advise you to believe that with breathing you can also inhale self-confidence. You are the only person who needs to believe this will work. Soon you won't just believe this. You will have proved this to yourself.

> *"I have an important meeting with someone in a few days and I'm so afraid that I will mess it up," someone said to me on the telephone. "A friend of mind told me that you helped him in a similar situation. But nothing my friend said to me was helpful. What would you suggest?"*
>
> *"You are breathing right now, aren't you?" I asked him.*
>
> *"Of course I am," he replied. "But so what?"*
>
> *"Right now, begin your practice of breathing in self-confidence with every intake of oxygen."*
>
> *"Look here," he complained, "I've been breathing my entire life and it hasn't increased my self-confidence."*
>
> *"Of course not," I agreed. "It's because you haven't yet practiced*

giving your mind the suggestion that each and every breath will increase your self-confidence."

"That's correct," he agreed. "I haven't."

"From now on when you want more self-confidence repeat to yourself, 'I am increasing my self-confidence with each and every breath.' Say this with enthusiasm and passion! Say this with intensity! Keep repeating, 'I am increasing my self-confidence with each and every breath,' as intensely as you can. Repeating it with intensity is a powerful self-suggestion."

He later reported, "I did what you suggested. Right before the meeting I said it as intensely as I have ever said anything: With each breath I am becoming more and more self-confident. And I did."

34

COMMITMENT AND DETERMINATION

A strong sense of commitment and determination is the foundation for every highly successful person. In any field of endeavor, those who are highly committed and determined to succeed have a tremendous advantage over anyone who lacks commitment and determination.

The Torah ideal of self-confidence is not competition with others. In fact, self-confidence allows every person to be totally committed and determined to being the best person that he can be.

You don't need to be more self-confident than anyone else. You just need to be self-confident in your own way, to carry you further along your journey on your life's mission.

Decide to be totally committed and determined to keep developing your self-confidence. When this attitude is internalized and integrated, you will find many opportunities to continually develop in your unique way.

When you hear someone speak, listen for ideas and tools to help you gain self-confidence. You will have your own insights in what you personally can do. When you read, your mind will pick up on ideas that readers without a similar commitment will pass over and not notice.

When you are totally committed and determined to keep developing your self-confidence, you will learn more from every self-confident person you meet. And when you encounter someone who lacks self-confidence, you might realize how this person could increase his self-confidence. Perhaps you can show this book to that person. But even if you cannot help him, you will be able to learn something about what you could do to improve your own self-confidence.

Look at every person you encounter as another Divinely sent messenger to help you keep building your self-confidence.

I was told by someone, "I couldn't understand why I wasn't more successful in reaching my goals. I did reach some of my more minor goals, but the really big goals that would have made a major difference in my life seemed to be totally elusive. Eventually I spoke to someone who had a reputation for helping people reach what they call 'Wow goals,' the goals that make you say, 'WOW! That would be awesome!'

"He questioned me and then said, "I see that you are sincere about wanting to reach those goals. But you are missing one major ingredient: an intense commitment to do whatever it takes. Yes, you feel it would really be great if you reached your goals. But people who put their entire heart and soul into their goals have a much better chance of reaching them. Some people call this a P.I.C., a personal internal

commitment. The energy of those who have this is way beyond the energy of those who have a less determined wish to accomplish and achieve.'"

The fellow told me, "I finally understood what I was missing. When I intensified my inner commitment to do all that I could do, I made breakthroughs that I never thought possible."

35

A SENSE OF HUMOR CAN HAVE A MAJOR POSITIVE IMPACT

Humor has proven to be an effective tool that can be used to change the way you think about things. Saying something funny or exaggerated is not meant to portray an accurate portrait of your present level of self-confidence. Rather, it is a direction of improvement. You are conditioning your mind to make future self-confidence more of a possibility in your own unique way.

In the most enthusiastic and humorous tone of voice that your dramatic ability allows, repeat the following exaggerated claim:

"I have amazing, awe-inspiring, awesome, blissful, breathtaking, championshiplike, ecstatic, energetic, euphoric, fabulous, gigantic, glorious, intense, joyful, magical, magnificent, marvelous, massive, miraculous, stupendous, terrific, total, tremendous, unbelievable, universal, unstoppable, vibrant, victorious, and vigorous self-confidence."

The more you repeat the humorous claim, the more the contrast of normal and reachable levels of positive self-confidence will seem feasible for you.

Someone who tried for a long time to upgrade his self-confidence was totally discouraged.

"Nothing seems to be working for me," he said sadly. "I've tried and tried, and no matter what I've done, it hasn't worked."

This fellow was very serious about everything. I thought a more humorous approach might be more effective.

"I have a suggestion to make," I said to him. "Please do me a favor and experiment. This approach is the exact opposite of seriously trying to increase your self-confidence. Are you willing to give it a fair chance?"

He reluctantly agreed.

"I want you to repeat after me, with all your heart and all your soul, using your most upbeat tone of voice as if you were reciting a powerful cheer: 'I have amazing, awe-inspiring, awesome, blissful, breathtaking, championshiplike, ecstatic, energetic, euphoric, fabulous, gigantic, glorious, intense, joyful, magical, magnificent, marvelous, massive, miraculous, stupendous, terrific, total, tremendous, unbelievable, universal, unstoppable, vibrant, victorious, and vigorous self-confidence.'"

The fellow burst out laughing as he repeated this after me, then said, "But I can't say that!"

"You just did," I argued.

"But it's not true!" he exclaimed.

"I didn't claim it's true," I agreed. "It's not true for you and it's not true for me. But if you repeat this highly exaggerated proclama-

tion over and over again, it will make a real difference in your actual self-confidence. A practical level of self-confidence will seem reasonable after this!"

Laughing, the fellow said that although he still feels that this is ridiculous, he could see it working for him.

36

BLAME KEEPS SELF-CONFIDENCE THE SAME

Some people have developed the habit of blaming others for their lack of self-confidence. Parents, teachers, siblings, class-mates, neighbors have all been blamed for causing people to have low self-confidence levels. But right now you have the self-confidence that you have and you don't have the self-confidence that you don't have. This is your present reality, regardless of the potential to lay blame.

Blaming someone else claims that someone else is in charge of your mind, which creates self-confidence. When you were a young child other people's opinions had a major impact on your life. And it's understandable that what you thought when you were young influenced the way you are now. But you now have a greater understanding that you can take charge and create self-confidence right this moment.

How do you stop blaming someone else? By thinking thoughts

that are inconsistent with blaming. Thoughts of blame create resentment and negative feelings. Grateful thoughts create positive feelings and enable you to access more resourceful states of mind. For example, you can think right now, *I am reading about increasing my level of self-confidence. I am grateful that I can see. I am grateful that I can read. I am grateful for everyone who had a part in teaching me how to read. I am grateful that I am breathing now. And I am grateful I am alive.*

From this place of gratitude, your state of mind will be better. It will be easier for you to think of ideas and ways to build your self-confidence.

In short, blaming a situation or a person for any lack of self-confidence prevents you from doing what you can to increase your self-confidence. Don't blame yourself for this pattern. Just make the wisest choice of thoughts, words, and actions right now.

"I used to be a blamer," a former addict with low self-confidence told me. "I suffered from a number of addictions. Was it my fault? Not in my mind. I considered my lack of self-confidence to be at the root of my addictions. I tried to drown my feelings of inferiority by doing things that temporarily made me feel better. Did this work well? Not really. It just covered up my bad feelings with temporary solutions that were not really solutions.

"Then one day a true friend said to me, 'You blame your problems on your controlling parents. But let me tell you the truth. Only when you take full responsibility for your thoughts, feelings, words, and actions will you develop the self-control that will really make a major positive shift in your life.' He spoke from the bottom of his heart. The truth of what he said hit home.

"Once I gave up blaming and realized it was up to me, with the Almighty's help I was able to make the wisest choices, one day at a time.

"I am now free from blaming. And while I still struggle at times, my personal responsibility has enabled me to be victorious over my previous harmful habits. It's like I am living a totally new life."

37

SELF-CONFIDENT PEOPLE ARE THANKFUL FOR HONEST FEEDBACK

Honest feedback helps you improve. This is true for every area of our lives, especially the important ones. Positive feedback is usually more pleasant than negative feedback. But people who sincerely want to improve are grateful for any feedback that will enable them to become a better person and to improve important skills. Because feedback can be tremendously helpful, self-confident people are grateful and thankful for honest feedback. This is so even when they would have preferred a compliment.

People giving feedback have a responsibility to do so in a positive manner. Both the tone of voice and the content of what is said should convey the message, "I care about you and I want you to do well." But the more self-confident a person is, the more easily he can appreciate critical feedback, even if it was not worded as diplomatically as it could have been.

If you tend to be a bit rough or tough when you give feedback, you need feedback on how you give feedback. If you see that people are not as grateful for your feedback as they might be, perhaps you should consult someone who is a sensitive communicator. You could say, "I would like to have a positive influence on more people. Can you suggest how to do that in a way that the person I give feedback to will appreciate it?"

"I considered myself very self-confident," someone I interviewed told me. "But I hated criticism of any kind. I always assumed that anyone who gave me negative feedback was just being mean. I automatically ignored anything that wasn't totally positive.

"But one day someone pointed out that if I really wanted to improve in important areas, I would be more open to hearing honest feedback and not only praise. He explained that not everyone knows how to wisely differentiate between making helpful and counterproductive comments, but I would be wise to develop a more positive attitude toward feedback that could be highly beneficial for me.

"I had to be honest with myself. I would gain immensely from accepting critical feedback. The pain is temporary but the benefits can be eternal. This openness to feedback made a major positive difference in my life."

38

LACK OF SELF-CONFIDENCE CAN BE A GREAT OPPORTUNITY

Any time you become aware that you lack self-confidence, you have another wonderful opportunity to build your self-confidence.

Lack of self-confidence is not a real problem. It's just a temporary state of mind. When you stop thinking that you can't say or do something only because you lack the confidence to do it, you realize you can say or do anything! It's just a matter of letting go of an imaginary block.

Realizing that the block is imaginary releases your mind and you feel an inner calm. You don't even need to access a self-confident state!

Feeling a lack of self-confidence can remind your conscious mind that you really can be as self-confident as you would like to be. In other words, letting go of a lack of self-confidence can open the road toward enhancing your life.

It's wonderful to know that any thought or feeling of a lack of self-confidence can immediately be transformed into a thought or feeling of personal development!

As you remember any past situation in which you didn't have the self-confidence you wanted, you can imagine having that self-confidence. Your memories of actual events can trigger your life-enhancing imagination. This is a great pattern to have. And by using your imagination right now, this pattern is yours for a lifetime.

In the beginning you might have to remember that you have this thought pattern available. But after applying it a number of times, you won't need to remember it; you will automatically remember to use these opportunities to enhance your self-confidence.

At a self-development workshop, I suggested a wonderful exercise to build self-confidence. Everyone was to imagine past situations when he didn't speak up or take action because of a lack of self-confidence. Now everyone would picture himself being super confident in similar situations.

One man later commented, "I used to feel bad every time I remembered certain moments of how I limited myself by lacking sufficient self-confidence. I thought that I would always feel distressed by the memories. But after this exercise, I realized that those same memories could serve as a resource for seeing myself having super confidence. It was amazing to see how this exercise enabled me to transform a great liability into a powerful asset."

39

EMPOWERED MEMORIES

A s you remember a specific memory of feeling empowered, recall what you saw, what you said, and how you felt. Allow yourself to feel those feelings right now. All you need is just one memory of feeling empowered, a moment when you spoke or acted with a feeling of inner strength.

Recall a moment when you felt you were able to say or do something that needed a sense of empowerment. Even if you didn't realize it at the time, this moment of empowerment meant your self-confidence was high. You might not have been thinking at all about your self-confidence; your focus was on the content of what you wanted to say and the actions you were about to take.

By being calmly persistent, eventually you will be able to recall at will a time that you were empowered. Having many memories of times you felt empowered will make it easier for you to access an empowered state when you need it the most.

Imagine that a professional photographer was present whenever you felt empowered. He took pictures of the look on your face and of the entire scene. So you have pictures of your expression and what you saw at that time. Imagine having an entire mental wall filled with these empowered pictures.

Since these pictures are in your own mind, you can create imaginary scenes in your imagination. Imagine that you are in a gigantic room filled with photographs of your empowered moments. Pictures of being empowered are displayed in every direction. Just looking at these pictures fills your consciousness with a strong sense of empowerment. An empowered state is a high state of self-confidence. Allow yourself to feel these feelings now.

I mentioned in a class I was giving that I was writing a book on self-confidence. An attendee approached me later and said, "I look forward to reading your book. I lack self-confidence to such a degree that it's difficult to imagine that a book would actually help me."

"Can you remember times when you did feel self-confident?" I asked.

"Yes, but they were few and far between. Even when I did feel more confident than usual, those feelings weren't very strong," he admitted.

"Can you think of anyone you ever saw in person, or even someone you have heard of, that you consider very empowered?" I asked him.

"Yes," he replied. "As a matter of fact, I have a specific person in mind. He is extremely self-confident. His dynamic energy helps others become more motivated to do things that they wouldn't have been able to do otherwise."

"Great! Now imagine that you are this person."

"I can't. It's way beyond my reality," he protested.

"So imagine that you are in his presence, and that he is using all of his powers to empower you for the next minute."

"I can do that," the fellow said with a big smile on his face.

"Now double this image in size and feel your own energy increasing."

You could tell from this fellow's body language that he was feeling stronger.

"Now imagine that you were doubling the intensity of this scene and then double it once again."

His facial expression and his body language kept getting stronger.

"Now say with me, 'I am getting stronger and stronger and even stronger than that.'"

We repeated this phrase together. Each repetition was stronger than the last.

"I feel stronger now than I can ever remember feeling," he said.

"Great. Now remember this moment. Give it a name and whenever you want to experience this feeling again, recall that name. For example, you can say, 'Now I will allow myself to enter my super-confident empowered state.' Keep practicing in an intense tone of voice and it will become easier for you to access this state at will."

40

CLIMBING YOUR EMOTIONAL-SPIRITUAL LADDER

My teachers used to say that we are always on an emotional-spiritual ladder. We constantly go up and down. Every positive thought, word, and action takes us up higher. Keep going in the right direction. This is the message of Jacob's prophetic dream of the ladder to Heaven.

Not every thought, word, and action has the same significance. But every thought, word, and action is either a step up or a step down. With an actual stepladder, you can only go one step at a time. But on the emotional-spiritual ladder you can fly up to the highest rung with one elevating thought, one empowering conversation, or one life-transforming action.

You raise yourself spiritually with each spiritual thought, word, and action. Let this thought increase your self-confidence. Focusing on insecure thoughts robs you of your self-confidence. It is a step in the wrong direction. It moves you lower down your ladder.

If you keep traveling and are headed in the right direction, eventually you will reach your destination. If you are going in the wrong direction, you won't get where you want to go, no matter how long you continue traveling that way. Don't waste time being upset. Turn around and take the next step in the right direction. Even if you progress slowly, when you are persistent you will go far.

By raising your level of self-confidence, you will find it easier to make better choices. Higher levels of self-confidence will open up more possibilities of what you can do to climb your ladder. Ask yourself, *Will this choice take me up my ladder or not?*

Each person's ladder is unique. You are never in a contest with others. Who can climb higher or faster is only valid in a physical race. When it comes to your spiritual ladder, every step higher can be a source of joy.

I thought about how the idea of climbing a spiritual ladder can be utilized by many people on a daily level. Then I realized that most people walk up and down stairs every day. Each staircase gives them many opportunities to reduce their stress by becoming calmer and more open to increasing their self-confidence.

I told someone today, "Every time you walk up steps today, repeat to yourself, 'Every step I take will increase my self-confidence.' And when you walk down steps, you can say to yourself, 'Each step I take walking down will make me calmer and calmer.'"

With a gigantic smile on his face, he shook my hand and said, "Just hearing that from you now has enriched my life." When I saw him again a few hours later, he said that the powerful idea was still on his mind.

41

AN IMAGINARY FRIEND FOR ADULTS

Anyone with an imagination can imagine a tremendously self-confident mentor who appears whenever you need him. As children we all had the ability to create an imaginary friend. Some people keep this ability their entire lives. Others need to revive this tool that had not been utilized for a long time. But everyone can really benefit from having an imaginary friend as a self-confidence coach.

Imagine an expert at self-confidence who goes with you wherever you go. He whispers self-confident messages into your inner ear. He consistently tells you things like, "You can do it," "This will be fun," "It's easier than you think," "I know you better than you know yourself, and I know you have the ability to say and do this even though you might think you can't."

This works so well because the entire problem of a lack of self-confidence is only an imaginary problem! It was created by the self-talk in your mind. Since its imagination that creates the problem, imagination can overcome it.

Some people convinced themselves long ago that they lack self-confidence. They might argue, "What do you mean that my lack of self-confidence is only in my imagination? I know it's real. I really do lack self-confidence." Anyone who has been repeating this myth to themselves long enough really believes it's true. Believing it is true creates a feeling that is consistent with that belief.

Realizing that the belief is not reality is a major step to overcoming a lack of self-confidence. People who have hired self-confidence coaches have found that a powerful and authoritative self-confidence coach was able to help them overcome this strong but imaginary limitation. If you have the resources to hire an expensive self-confidence coach, it might be worthwhile to do so. But an imaginary self-confidence coach doesn't cost anything. You don't even need to make a telephone call. You just imagine it. And you can imagine a powerful self-confidence coach right this very moment.

If you have a vivid imagination, you can imagine your coach is anyone you know or anyone you have read about. You can take a real historical figure or someone imaginary to use as your self-confidence coach.

You don't even need to visualize the person. You can just hear his voice whispering into your ear. If you would prefer, your imaginary coach can shout in a loud and clear booming voice that only you can hear.

Some people already do this. Others might create all kinds of make-believe excuses why they can't use their imaginations to help themselves. Some even claim that it would be wrong to do this. But this obstacle is only an imaginary obstacle. Since you are going to use this for a beneficial purpose, you may use your imagination in this way. If you are concerned that others might laugh at or make fun of you for doing this, don't tell anyone. It's normal for people to have the self-confidence they need. So no one needs to know that you are using your imagination to create an imaginary self-confidence coach.

As long as you use your Divinely given intelligence and common sense to apply this only in safe and secure ways, it makes sense to make use of your imagination in this creative way. Your only limit is the limit of your own imagination.

I was recently faced with a situation that I found challenging: I had committed to make five difficult telephone calls on behalf of someone important to me. I was afraid that I would chicken out but I didn't want to make up a story to explain, "It was too hard for me to do it. I'm sorry to let you down."

As I reread this chapter during the editing process, my inner coach told me the truth. "You, like everyone else, can really do anything you sincerely are determined to do. The difficulty is only an imaginary difficulty. Visualize yourself enjoying making those calls. This will be a great resource for the rest of your life, and you will be helping your friend. So intensify your will to do it."

As my inner coach said this to me, I decided, "Whether I actually find this easy to do or difficult to do, I'm doing it. Consider it done!"

42
THOUGHTS OF INSECURITY

Many people think they have valid reasons for feeling insecure. They can tell you many reasons why they are entitled to feel insecure. But formerly insecure people who changed their thinking and their entire attitudes have told me, "Now I realize that it was only because I was thinking insecure thoughts that I felt insecure."

When someone stops thinking insecurely, they stop feeling insecure. But you can't completely stop thinking. As long as we are alive, our minds think one thought after the other. You can't control a thought that you already thought, so let the insecure thoughts just flow by. You have free will to choose your next thought. So choose a thought that will enhance your life and create a better mood.

A school principal taught the idea of choosing thoughts to his elementary school students. Many of them are more open to this concept than adults.

It's really common sense. We've been thinking one thought after the other our entire lives. When you think about a topic or subject that you find fascinating, your mind automatically puts you into a more lively state.

Some people "get it" after hearing this concept just once. "Yes, I hear what you are trying to teach me," they say. "Any insecurity I feel is caused by thinking insecure thoughts. As I choose to think in a more constructive manner, I will feel much better about myself and my life. I can see how this will change my life. Just saying this has an immediate positive effect on me."

Other people need to hear this idea many times. They might hear this from one person but it doesn't register. But when they hear it later from someone else, it suddenly makes sense.

Not feeling insecure isn't as positive as feeling self-confident, but it's a lot better than experiencing the discomfort of insecure feelings. For many people it is a step in the right direction. After not thinking insecure thoughts, they are more open to start thinking with self-confidence.

I met a social worker who had heard a lecture by Syd Banks. It changed his entire approach to dealing with inmates of high-security prisons, with poverty-stricken homeless people, with addicts of many types, and with high-powered stressed-out executives.

Syd Banks only had a ninth-grade education when he dropped out of school. He earned a living as a welder, but felt insecure. Someone commented that he only felt insecure because of his insecure thoughts.

Syd Banks suddenly realized that the answer to his insecurity was totally dependent on his own thoughts. If he stopped thinking inse-

cure thoughts he wouldn't feel insecure feelings. This is at the root of all stress.

Stop thinking stressful thoughts and you won't feel stressed out. Stop thinking angry thoughts and you won't experience angry feelings.

It's easy to say, but many people just superficially nod in agreement and continue to think the same thoughts that made them feel insecure, stressed, and angry. But those who really understand the full ramifications and consequences of internalizing this message live much calmer and more self-confident lives. They realize that our natural emotional state is a state of well-being and inner calm. Distressful thoughts create distress.

Even before mastering thoughts of appreciation and gratitude, just letting go of distressful thoughts will free a person from insecurity and distress.

43

YOUR FOCUS BECOMES YOUR REALITY

We all have had many experiences when we felt self-confident and many moments when we didn't. Self-confident people focus more on the times and moments when they were self-confident.

We all have had successful moments and less successful moments. Self-confident people focus more on their successes. People who lack self-confidence tend to do the opposite.

Regardless of your earlier focus, right now you can resolve to keep your main focus on your successes and on when you felt self-confident.

Being self-confident does not mean that you never feel the opposite of self-confidence. Focusing on your successes does not mean that you deny your less successful experiences. But focusing on the reality that you would like to reinforce will keep your mind on the positive thoughts and feelings that improve your life.

Our total reality includes everything that we've experienced since day one. But it's impossible to keep everything in mind in any one moment. We are always selective, choosing what to keep in mind at any time. It only takes common sense to recognize that it's wiser to focus on our successes and our moments of self-confidence to become even more self-confident. If a negative thought comes to mind, choose to focus on something positive.

When you make mistakes, think about what you need to know and do to prevent those and similar mistakes from happening again. If you don't know the answers, consult someone who does. Practice the correct way of doing things and focus on those corrections. In many areas of your life, you probably already do this. Do it even more, in more areas.

Repeat to yourself a number of times, *I will keep my main focus on the reality that I want for myself. I will keep my main focus on my successes. I will keep my main focus on my moments of self-confidence.*

Your self-affirmations become more powerful every time you repeat them. Even after you have integrated a positive pattern, additional repetitions may make them even stronger. This is especially important if you find yourself unwittingly repeating negative self-statements. Override them with your focus on your goals.

I recall how a certain student reacted with great irritation when I suggested that he change his focus. "Reality is reality," he insisted. "Reality just happens to be the way things really are. Your focus doesn't change reality."

"Are you satisfied with living in what you claim is your reality?" I asked.

"Of course not!" he replied. "But the fact that I'm dissatisfied with my reality doesn't change things."

"I agree with what you just said. Dissatisfaction doesn't automatically make things better. The key word is FOCUS! Your focus is powerful. By changing what your mind focuses on, you change your entire life.

"Your personal reality is created by your personal focus. Many people fail to realize this. An objective observation will show you the truth of the power of your focus.

"Those who have mastered their ability to focus on moments that support their goals have totally transformed their lives. You too can master this. This concept is too valuable to just argue about and not even attempt to make your new reality. Do me a favor and test it out for yourself. Those who did try it out have upgraded their quality of life."

44

WHEN SOMEONE IMPORTANT DOESN'T BELIEVE IN YOU

It's easier to have self-confidence when other people believe in you. It's more challenging to have self-confidence when someone important to you doesn't believe in you. But authentic self-confidence is an inside job. When you truly believe in your abilities, talents, and inner strengths, you can still maintain self-confidence even when someone else fails to believe in you.

We need to be honest with ourselves. Is there a valid reason why someone who is important to us doesn't believe in us? We can ask that person what to do to grow and improve.

But very often someone else's lack of belief in us is a shortcoming in that person's own mind. It does not reflect our true value and worth, and it does not reflect our true abilities and potential.

Self-confidence is what you believe about yourself. If you stop believing in yourself because of someone else's disbelief, then you are allowing someone to rob you of your self-confidence.

Ask the Almighty for His help in letting your self-confidence become stronger and stronger. Pray for the intelligence to know the wisest thing to do next. Pray for Divine help in becoming all that you can become and doing all that you can do. Believe in the Almighty's power to give you the self-confidence that you need in challenging times and moments.

Throughout history there have been many people who overcame the doubts and skepticism of others to become more than what others thought possible. You can choose to be one of them. Intense self-confidence can create "miracles" in one's life.

The way you talk to yourself about your self-confidence is really more important than someone else's opinion. Strengthen the power of your imagination by visualizing your self-confidence becoming stronger and stronger. Repeat this truth to yourself over and over again in order to internalize it: *My self-confidence is up to me. It's great when others help me build my self-confidence. But ultimately it's my own belief in myself that counts.*

By giving up, you guarantee that you won't achieve and accomplish what you could if instead you intensified your will. Having self-confidence won't always be sufficient. But without self-confidence you will be needlessly limiting yourself.

Some people are afraid that if they have too much self-confidence, they will suffer disappointment. But if you are truly doing all that you can do, you can be satisfied knowing that you did all you could before discovering it's impossible. Don't let challenges stop you if you can overcome them. Feel intense pleasure in knowing that you are making an honest effort to do all you can.

Someone I knew who had accomplished much in life was asked by an interviewer, "Did your parents believe in you as a child?"

His answer surprised the listeners. He said, "My father expressed his belief in me way beyond my belief in myself. Unfortunately, I considered his positive statement as a total exaggeration.

"On the other hand, my mother used to say to me that it's too bad that I wasn't blessed with the great mind of my father. I didn't feel bad about her saying this. I agreed with her and viewed this as a statement of a true fact.

"As I got older and developed myself, I realized that although I did not have my father's brilliance in many areas, I had my own strengths and talents. My mother eventually acknowledged that I had surpassed her hopes and expectations. But by then I recognized my unique skills, so while I appreciated my mother's positive comments, I didn't have a real need for them on a practical level."

45

SELF-CONFIDENT PEOPLE CAN FEEL NERVOUS

The more self-confident someone is, the less nervous he tends to be. Nevertheless, it is very normal to feel nervous sometimes. Most people are nervous at some point, but those with self-confidence don't allow their nerves to hold them back. Don't be nervous about being nervous. You can just notice it and move on.

People who lack self-confidence tell themselves negative stories about being nervous. *If I'm nervous it means that I lack self-confidence,* they might say. *If I'm nervous it means I lack self-esteem. It means that I don't really love myself. It means that I don't have enough trust in Hashem. It means that I'm an awful person. It means that I am doomed to be a failure in life.*

Of course, not every insecure person takes it to this extreme. The really good news is that if anyone reading this section is thinking, *That's me. I sometimes think these and similar thoughts,* he has the ability to stop himself from thinking this way right now.

Instead, he can think, *I'm glad that I'm reading a book about self-confidence right this moment. I can choose to think more self-confident thoughts right now. Even if I told myself negative stories about being nervous in the past, right now I choose to be more optimistic about my future. Right now, I will imagine how great I will feel when I increase my self-confidence. Right now, I will have so much self-confidence that any nervousness will act as a reminder that I can increase my self-confidence. The fact that I am nervous means that I am alive. And whenever I remember that I am alive, I feel great joy in reflecting on all the good that I can do.*

You can decrease your nervousness by increasing your self-confidence. You can also decrease your nervousness by applying L.S.D.: laughing, singing, and dancing. L.S.D. is not directly related to self-confidence. But all three actions can enable a person to access a better emotional state by changing your biochemistry and putting you in a more pleasant state. The more spiritual the song and the dance, the more elevated you feel.

In *Serenity* (ArtScroll, 2001), you can find many ideas and stories about decreasing stress and increasing an inner calm. Serene people find it easier to be self-confident. And even if they aren't self-confident, they will find it easier to be calm about that state.

"I used to think I lacked self-confidence," a wealthy person once told me, "until I heard an extremely wealthy investment banker speak at a banquet. The organization was honoring him for supporting their cause. He was totally confident in his ability to make intelligent choices when it came to investing money. But he was very nervous about speaking in public.

"He apologized for being so nervous. He even made a joke out of it. He said that if he felt as nervous about investments as he did about speaking, he would look for a new job. He read his boring speech without making eye contact with the audience.

"I knew that I could speak in public much better than he could, even though I didn't have a fraction of his financial success. From then on I was much less stressed about my own nervousness," he concluded.

46

CRITICAL PEOPLE

Some people tend to be very critical of everybody. Some people tend to see the good in others. Some people tend to see the innocence in others. Some people want others to succeed. Some people want others to fail. More spiritual people have a more spiritual outlook on life and on other people.

The more self-confident someone is, the less it matters to him what others will think. A self-confident person who is also a spiritual person will focus more on doing the right thing, on being kind, on being elevated, on being a servant of the Creator. Such a person won't try to win the approval of those who don't care about doing the right thing, or those who aren't kind or are far from being elevated, or those who aren't concerned with the will of the Creator.

As we grow older, we realize that it is not worth worrying about whether or not these people approve of us. Their approval doesn't make a bit of a difference in our lives. Of course, we must be kind and compassionate to such people. But really caring about their momentary approval or disapproval is a waste of time.

Spiritual, self-confident people know that time is precious. Time is a limited commodity. Time is well spent on Torah study, prayer, kindness, character development, and other spiritual aspects of life, such as caring for one's health and well-being. There is no place in a spiritual, self-confident person's mind for irrelevant and unimportant matters; his mind is too busy to be overly concerned with, *I wonder what other people are thinking of me.*

We all need the approval of some people for practical and constructive purposes. But if we are speaking and acting kindly and compassionately, and behave in a way consistent with true Torah ideals, we need to be open to the beneficial feedback of others. But the criticism of needlessly critical people can be gently dismissed from our minds. It might be momentarily uncomfortable to hear, but we won't give it too much thought. This gives a great deal of mental freedom to those who master this ability.

"I used to be very intimidated by critical people," someone told me, "but then I had a realization that freed me. I heard a talk about nargonim [critical people]. These people find fault with everything: other people, the food, the weather, anyone who tries to do things for them, stores, books, and everything else. They are not satisfied or content. If there is anything to complain about, they will focus on it and complain.

"But the people they harm the most, without realizing it, are themselves. They are never satisfied or happy. Yes, they enjoy the power they feel when they complain. But the price is that they are

unliked by others. People try to avoid them. They have problems in marriage and with their children. They have problems when it comes to working with anyone else. They are totally miserable all the time. Often they are arrogant and conceited and try to hide how unhappy they really are.

"I said to myself, 'These people rob themselves of a good life. They think they are smart and clever. But they really are emotionally dumb. I began to have sympathy for them, but I was never again intimidated. Those who lack emotional intelligence are greatly handicapped. This awareness let me look much more objectively at what they said, and the real quality of life of the person who said it.'"

47 ━━━━━━━━━━━━━━━━━━━━━━

HAVING A DIFFICULT DAY

Everyone has days they consider difficult. Some people have them more often and some have them less often. Sometimes a day can be so difficult that everyone would consider it difficult. You might be reading this chapter on a day that you find difficult. Gratitude makes it is easier to cope with these hard days.

A difficult day is just one day in a person's life. It's not the complete picture of one's life. Even if a person has many difficult days, he can develop greater self-confidence by thinking wisely about his life.

Every day can be viewed as having many opportunities for moments of spiritual greatness. From this perspective, the more difficult the day, the greater you become when you think, speak, and act at your best for the way you are feeling at the time.

Joyful days are more fun than difficult days. Serene days are more conducive to feelings of well-being. Peaceful days are pleasant. But our soul has opportunities to be elevated regardless of the type of day.

Just as every season of the year is unique, so too every day of life has special aspects. Some people tend to keep judging days as easy or difficult. But it's preferable to not judge the entire day at once; you only need to think about this moment, one moment at a time.

Since we live each day moment by moment, we only need to actually choose how to think, speak, and act in the given moment. In that moment it doesn't really matter how the previous moments of that day were, or how later moments of the day will eventually be. We have free will to choose our next thought, or word, or action just for that moment. Having self-confidence in the intelligence and wisdom the Creator gives us at that moment will help us make better choices.

People have told me that when they are having difficult days, they consciously think about things that made them feel better. Some recall laughing at things they found funny. This brings a smile to their face and creates a biochemistry that makes them feel better when they're having a hard time.

Ask people, "How do you deal with difficult days? What have other people said helps them deal with days they find difficult?"

Some people told me, "Some of the most interesting and exciting days in my life were days that I at first found difficult. They turned out to be much better than I would have imagined."

I have heard from other people, "Even if I found a specific day difficult, I know from experience that a good night's sleep will help me wake up refreshed the next day. Feeling better, I feel more self-confident that I will be able to think of solutions for the aspects of the day that I found difficult. At other times, new and better perspectives have helped me transform the way I was looking at an experience that was originally challenging for me."

Perhaps this will be true for you also.

"How do you deal with difficult days?" I asked someone who was very spiritual.

"Difficult days?" he asked with a puzzled look on his face. "There aren't difficult days. There are just days that are more challenging and days that are less challenging. The difficulties about any given situation or day are just the way a person's mind perceives that situation or day. I realize that all is for my ultimate good. A greater challenge gives me greater opportunity to continue to develop my character traits. I don't ask for challenges. I'm not on that level. But I realize that it's up to me to make it easier and more enjoyable or to make it seem more difficult. This awareness makes it easier for me to cope with whatever Hashem sends my way."

48

"I'M NOT SELF-CONFIDENT BECAUSE I EXPLAIN WHY I'M NOT SELF-CONFIDENT"

People who think they lack self-confidence can usually come up with valid reasons why they are not self-confident. They can blame their intelligence, their life circumstances, their financial situation, their parents, their teachers, their friends and relatives, their lack of skills and talents, the feedback they heard from others, and many other reasons.

Any of these reasons can be valid. But the reasons are not the real cause. It's the person's belief in any reason that creates a lack of self-confidence. The lack of self-confidence is caused by the self-talk giving reasons for not being self-confident.

There are people with similar circumstances who have the same level of intelligence, skills, and talents, but they are still self-confident. They believe in themselves in realistic ways. They know that it's not what people have said to them in the past that matters, but what they say to themselves in the present.

Affirmations work. Positive affirmations said sincerely and with belief will have a positive impact. Negative statements said sincerely and with belief will have a negative impact. Our thoughts about our self-confidence either serve as positive affirmations or negative confirmations. They cause us to create the way of being consistent with their message.

Once any individual realizes this with total clarity, he will be motivated to stop giving reasons for not being self-confident and start creating more self-confidence. He will realize, *I'm not self-confident because I explain why I'm not self-confident.*

Believe that you have a right to have self-confidence this very moment. This is an attitude based on your thoughts. These thoughts create feelings. Feeling self-confident allows you to practice the skills and talents and ways of being that will enhance your life.

Edit what you say to yourself right now. Instead of saying, *I'm not self-confident because …* you have a right to say, *I'm in the process of building my self-confidence. My self-confidence is getting stronger and stronger all the time.*

I personally feel good when I repeat this sentence. As a coach, I found that anyone who is willing to sincerely repeat this phrase and believe in the power of self-talk will improve his level of self-confidence. Here it is again:

"I'm in the process of building my self-confidence. My self-confidence is getting stronger and stronger all the time."

Someone started saying to me, "I'll tell you why I'm not self-confident. It's because …"

I had very good rapport with this person, so I interrupted him.

"Please do me a favor and don't say that," I said with a smile.

"Don't say what?" he asked. "I didn't finish my sentence."

"I might have let you finish your sentence, but you seem like the type of person who is willing to improve himself if something makes sense."

"Thank you for the compliment," he said. "You're right. I'm not interested in staying limited in my old ways of thinking. My goal is to keep developing myself. I'm very interested in what you want to tell me."

"Regardless of any reasons you tell yourself, just giving a reason for not being self-confident blocks your self-confidence.

"For two weeks, interrupt yourself if you are about to say anything that will needlessly limit your self-confidence. Keep telling yourself that you have just as much a right to self-confidence as any self-confident person who ever was, who is now, and who might be in the future. From now on, identify yourself as a person who is already self-confident about his ability to become even more self-confident. Keep telling yourself, 'My self-confidence keeps on growing each and every day for the rest of my life.' Let's see how this will impact your self-image."

He was willing to give this a try. He thanked me profusely for interrupting him because he immediately understood that he would benefit from this way of thinking. And he did.

49
CONSTANTLY TRY TO IMPROVE

People who consistently improve every day don't worry about their level of self-confidence. They focus on bettering whatever skill, talent, trait, and way of being is important to them.

Focus creates expertise. People who focus on a lack of self-confidence are focusing on the wrong thing. People who focus on how awful it is that they have so many problems become experts at finding problems. Wiser people might start off the same way, but they focus on what they need to do to find solutions. Focusing on solutions makes a person an expert at finding solutions.

People who focus on their lack of self-esteem will always find reasons to lack self-esteem. On the other hand, people who focus on the greatness of being created in the image of the Creator always realize that they have innate value and worth. That is, they know that they had infinite value and worth from the moment they were born. They know they don't need to earn the right to consider themselves valuable human beings. They were valuable from day one, and this valuable feeling is with them all the time.

Even though we all have innate value and worth, some people make many mistakes. Some people focus on their mistakes and faults and talk about them frequently. And what is much worse, they think about them over and over again, instead of figuring out how to avoid making the same mistakes. This becomes their subjective reality.

The good news is that at any given moment we all have the ability to recognize our infinite value and worth. We can commit ourselves to focus on the potential of every human being to transform his identity and self-image. Anyone blessed with a mind that can choose what to think is able to decide to think and act in ways that create a better human being.

This decision doesn't need to take a long time. It's within all of us to change our focus. Right now, focus on the ground. Look down and see what's down there. Now, look up and see what's above you. How long did it take to change your focus from the floor to the ceiling or from the ground to the sky? This change of focus can happen in a moment. We can change our focus in life just as quickly.

Commit yourself to keep your focus on constant and never-ending improvement. Do so joyfully. Do so with gratitude that you are alive and have an active mind. Do so with the knowledge that as you focus on constant improvement, you will actually improve.

Be patient and persistent. As you focus on improving, you will see progress. Don't unreasonably judge yourself about the speed of your progress.

Progress builds self-confidence. And progress depends only on the thoughts and actions that you choose. The fact that you are reading this book is part of the process of making progress in building your self-confidence. You have the ability to mentally review the most helpful ideas you've read in any section. Enjoy thinking about them, and share the ideas you like with others.

An average student eventually accomplished much more than some of his smarter classmates. As an adult, he told a group of people, "Based on how I did in school, no one would have predicted that I would accomplish as much as I did. But one thing my father told me when I graduated high school stayed with me as a guiding light in my life. 'Slow and steady wins the race.' This is an old idea repeated by many. But I took it seriously. I resolved to keep improving each and every day. I would be persistent and would never quit. I wasn't competing with anyone else. I just wanted to be the best that I could be.

"I had a positive image of myself as a person who knew he would be improving each and every day. Even when my progress was very slow, I focused on the progress that I was making. I felt tremendous self-confidence because I felt certain that I would be successful in all the important areas of my life. This principle has worked for me and I know that it will work for anyone who is determined to make daily progress."

50

A SHOT OF CONFIDENCE

Sometimes a person looks at himself in a limited way, and that is the way others see him. But every once in a while something special happens that gives a person a shot of confidence. In a transformational moment he does something that takes great courage and is a total game changer in his life. That courage becomes an integral part of who he is. That act of courage gives him a shot of confidence.

A person might have been considered a mediocre student. But then he has a new teacher who sees something special in him. That teacher believes in that student. From then on, that student starts to believe in himself. Their interaction gave that student a shot of confidence.

A person might have seen himself as shy and withdrawn. But then one Purim *seudah* he became the life of the party. He was outgoing. He spoke in front of a crowd. He sang and danced with more energy than he ever had before. That Purim experience gave him a shot of confidence. He no longer saw himself as shy and never again needed an external boost of confidence. He realized that his confidence was inside his mind and soul. He was able to access a similar state whenever he chose to.

A fellow wanted to raise funds for a very worthy cause. But he always talked himself out of collecting money, even when he deeply believed in the cause and truly wanted to help. Then he met someone who taught him how to fund-raise. That person role-played with him and had the fellow ask for large sums of money over and over again. Since it was just make-believe, the fellow found it easy to do. Then he had a sudden awareness: There is no practical difference between pretending to be a fund-raiser and actually asking others for money for a worthy cause. He tried it out in real life. To his surprise, the person he asked actually gave a large donation because he asked! That donation was a shot of confidence. It went to his mind, heart, and soul. From then on he found it easy and even enjoyable to raise money. He realized that he was able to do what he had thought was impossible for him. It changed his life forever.

If you lack confidence, realize that you are only missing a shot of confidence. There are many possible ways to obtain this shot. It might be from an external source or the ideas you read might wake you up to the possibility of becoming more self-confident than you ever imagined. And that moment might be this very moment. It gives me a great feeling to think that these sentences can make a major difference in even one person's life.

Someone with a very critical spouse once told me that because of the spouse's constant criticism, "I felt a total lack of confidence. I was told that whenever I explain anything, I am unclear. I was told that I am a very poor listener and that I am lazy and selfish. After hearing these critical messages over and over again, my self-confidence was at an all-time low. I thought my spouse's judgment was an accurate reflection of my capabilities, character traits, and potential.

"But fortunately I met someone professionally who had a much more objective view of me. This person was not critical of the way that I explained things, of the way I listened, and of my character traits. Instead, this person was a master at bringing out the strengths in people and giving a stream of positive feedback.

"I began to realize that the way anyone sees us has a lot to do with their own mindset and character traits. This positive person saw my strengths and enabled me to flourish in ways that I had not flourished before. I was able to improve in the areas that I had been criticized about. Now my spouse is much less critical than before and I've developed positive responses to critical feedback."

51

BEING UNDERESTIMATED NEEDN'T UNDERMINE YOUR SELF-CONFIDENCE

Some people take time to develop their intellectual abilities, their interpersonal skills, their creativity, and other inner strengths. Some people tend to be shy, quiet, and reserved. Some people don't show their full capacity until later on. It is easy for other people to underestimate their true abilities, talents, and skills.

Don't let someone who underestimates you determine your self-confidence. Realize that perhaps you haven't fully developed your inner strengths and skills. If you knew how capable you really are, you would have greater self-confidence. If you knew your true intelligence and your potential for creativity, you would have greater self-confidence.

Studies show the tremendous power of great teachers, mentors, and coaches. Their encouragement and support enable their students to achieve far beyond what most people expected of them.

Master teachers, mentors, and coaches see the potential of their students of all ages. They know how to bring out the best in people. They're not confused by their students' self-images and lack of confidence. They help the students see their potential, too.

Even if you don't have someone helping you bring out your best right now, be confident that you have much more potential than you think. Let this book serve as your mentor, coach, and teacher.

Your own self-confidence in the potential of the human spirit will enable you to grow. The more you develop your inner self, the more you will be able to do and accomplish.

Your personal success might teach those who underestimated you to have a greater belief in the potential of other people.

Someone was told he was learning disabled when he was 7 years old, and that he couldn't expect to do well academically. He dropped out of school when he was 13. He developed a few skills and was good at sports. But when he was 17, he met someone who saw his full potential. This person inspired him to see himself in a much more positive light. The mentor told him to repeat many times a day, "I am a genius and I apply my wisdom."

He found it hard to repeat this at first. But with practice it became easier and easier. Now in his mid-50s, the man is known as a brilliant master of many topics. He has read many books on many subjects. Besides teaching people how to make more money, he also lectures on a multitude of topics. He tells as many people as possible, "If I can do it, you can do it also."

52

THE ABILITY TO CHOOSE
YOUR NEXT THOUGHT

Machines that monitor brainwaves show that our brains are always active. Sometimes our thoughts flow one after another, even if we don't intend to think of anything at all. Other times we consciously choose what to think about.

Right now you can think of mountains. It might be Mount Everest. Or the Swiss Alps. Or the Rocky Mountains. Or mountains anywhere else in the world. After reading about mountains it will be easy for you to think about a mountain again in 15 seconds.

Right now you can choose another thought. You can choose to think of the name of your favorite song. You can even choose to think of five of your favorite songs.

When someone mentions a topic, you can choose to think about it. When you read something, it is easy to think about what those words are referring to.

Readers of this book will be thinking about self-confidence as they read about it. Readers of this section will have thought about mountains and about their favorite songs. The next sentence you will read here contains an extremely important idea.

"You have the ability to choose your next thought." You can't unthink a thought but you have the ability to choose your next thought. This is true right now. This will be true in an hour, in a day, in a week, in a month, and in a year. This is true for you at any time, all the time. You can actively choose the thoughts that you will be conscious of in your mind.

Let's try this out in the first person. *I have the ability to choose my next thought.* If you reflect on this sentence, you will be thinking thoughts connected to these words. This might empower you as it does many other people who have repeated it. *I have the ability to choose my next thought. That is great to know. This gives me a sense of hope and encouragement.*

You have the ability to think about moments of happiness and joy in the past. You have the ability to think about many more potential moments of happiness and joy. You have the ability to think about the good feelings you will feel if you become an expert at thinking about your moments of happiness and joy.

You have the ability to think about your calm and serene moments in the past or potential moments in the future. You might think of places where it would be easy for you to experience inner calm and serenity. Perhaps you have already read my book *Serenity* and can recall some of the ideas right now. You might think of people who are very calm and serene, and you might ask them how they developed or currently maintain this way of being.

You have the ability to think about many things that you are grateful for right now. You might think of what you have felt grateful for in the past. You might think of how wonderful your life will be when you become a master at thinking grateful thoughts.

You have the ability to think about when you felt moments of self-confidence. You might think of how wonderful it will be to master self-confidence. As you internalize the message of this section you will have a greater and deeper awareness of the truth in the statement, "I have the ability to choose my next thought."

Some people wonder how they can maintain thoughts and feelings of self-confidence. Many people realize that, "I have the ability to choose my next thought," means, "I don't need to worry about maintaining self-confidence. All I need to know is that at any given moment, I have the ability to think of thoughts that enable me to experience self-confidence. Since every single human being has had moments of self-confidence, at least when they were younger, everyone can access those thoughts and feelings right now. And so can I."

The more moments of self-confidence you experience, the easier it will be for you to choose this way of being right now and at any time in the future.

Someone recently challenged me, "Do you claim to always be self-confident?"

"No," I replied. "Sometimes I am and sometimes I'm not."

"Then how can you write a book on being self-confident?" he asked.

"That's easy to answer. I've already almost finished writing the book. Since I have many thoughts on the topic, I can type those thoughts on a computer."

"But you are being inconsistent," he challenged.

"That's right, I am," I confidently replied. "I can't undo any lack of self-confidence of the past. I won't try to do something that I know is impossible. But I can choose many self-confident moments in the future. If I write a book on the topic, many people will want to discuss the subject with me. I feel more self-confident when I talk about strengthening self-confidence. This helps me coach other people about becoming more self-confident. If someone wants to read a book whose author is always self-confident, this is not the book for him. But if he wants to read ideas that enabled the author to experience more self-confidence, then this is a book for him."

The fellow smiled and nodded his head. "I realize you are right. I would gain by reading and reviewing those ideas."

53

SELF-CONFIDENT ON THE OUTSIDE, INSECURE ON THE INSIDE

Some people project a self-confident image with the way they speak and behave, but on the inside they are really insecure. Therefore, you can't really know exactly how self-confident someone else really is. Authentic self-confidence is when a person feels comfortable about himself in his mind, regardless of whether or not he seems self-confident to others.

Insecurity might be obvious in a number of ways. Some people acknowledge their insecurity. But people who try to disguise their insecurity tend to deny any insecure thoughts or feelings.

The need to boast can demonstrate the speaker's insecurity. Insecurity drives him to tell others how great he is and to keep talking about his achievements, accomplishments, and plans to accomplish in the future.

Insecurity is also expressed when someone tries to belittle or make fun of others. Speaking against others or insulting people comes from a need to try to lift oneself up by putting others down. A truly self-confident person has no need to do this. If someone is authentically self-confident, he is happy to praise others and to make people feel good.

People who are secretly insecure are easier to anger. They react strongly to any slight to their honor or dignity. Their irritability causes others to feel uncomfortable around them.

Everyone is nervous sometimes. But people with high levels of insecurity are more nervous than others. Authentic self-confidence creates an inner calm. Self-confident people know that everyone is a valuable human being whether or not they succeed at any given task or project.

Individuals with high levels of self-confidence are willing to acknowledge that they are feeling nervous. They might know what they need to say and do. They might know that they are competent, even highly competent, but nevertheless they experience the normal reaction of human beings. This nervousness does not shake their self-confidence.

When asked if he is nervous, an insecure person trying to project an image of self-confidence might say, "No, I'm not nervous. Why should someone like me be nervous?"

He knows how insecure he actually feels inside, but he wants others to consider him self-confident, so he will deny his nervousness. Courage does not demand an absence of nervousness, but a willingness to speak up or to act despite feeling fear or being nervous.

The same is true regarding self-confidence. And with practice and greater degrees of competence, a person might eventually be totally calm and relaxed during situations when he used to be nervous.

There are many times when it is appropriate, even highly necessary, to project self-confidence on the outside even though you are feeling insecure inside. But be honest with yourself about how you are really feeling.

The goal of this book is not to help people pretend to be self-confident, but to actually create an honest attitude of self-confidence. True self-confidence can help you be confident about what you know and know how to do and to encourage you to want to gain more knowledge and higher levels of skill. When you feel insecure, you will do what you can to gain greater competence to earn the right to be confident about that matter.

You don't need to be an expert at something to be self-confident. You only need to believe in your own value as a person at all times, and in your ability to learn many more things in life.

Someone who appeared to very self-confident confided in me, "I have a major problem with self-confidence. I know that people assume I am self-confident. But deep down I am much more insecure than anyone can imagine. I feel awful about myself."

I reassured him, "I have known you for a long time and you have actually achieved a lot in life. You are comparing your feelings of insecurity with how you think others feel. I tell you with total certainty that a lot of other people who seem to be very self-confident are really much more insecure than you can imagine. It's normal to feel insecure. Many highly intelligent and highly competent individuals also experience feelings of insecurity.

"Where attention goes, energy flows. If you keep thinking about

how insecure you feel, you will increase your insecurity. Keep your major focus on gratitude for all the good in your life, and focus on the many acts of kindness that you can do. When you start to think about feeling insecure, let your profound gratitude for being alive be uppermost on your mind. This will make each day of your life more meaningful."

"Moreover," I continued, "you have actually experienced self-confidence many thousands of times. Often you take this for granted. From now on, whenever you start feeling insecure, remind yourself, 'I have the inner resource of self-confidence in many of my memories. That is what I will choose to focus on right now.'"

He later reported, "What you told me was incredibly helpful. I now spend much less time worrying about whether I am insecure or not, and much more time on gratitude. And yes, as you suggested, any insecure thoughts or feelings serve as a cue to remember times and moments when I did feel self-confident. This is great!"

54

IT'S NORMAL FOR SELF-CONFIDENCE TO RISE AND FALL

For most people, thoughts and feelings of self-confidence rise and fall. Some people don't experience a change in their level of self-confidence.

There are a number of reasons that someone's thoughts and feelings of self-confidence don't change. One explanation is that his self-confidence is always low, so it never goes up. Someone who thinks and feels this way could read this book a few times and eventually increase his self-confidence.

Another possibility is that this person's self-confidence is always very high. No matter what happens in his life or what someone says to him, his self-confidence is always high. No matter how well he does or how many mistakes he makes, his self-confidence is always high. No matter how fatigued or physically worn out he feels, his self-confidence is always high. No matter what the situation or circumstances, his self-confidence is always high.

Self-confidence might be such an integral part of a person's way of being that regardless of situations and circumstances, his thoughts and feelings of self-confidence remain stable. No matter what is going on in his life, no matter what time of the day or night, this super master of self-confidence always feels self-confident. Win or lose, whether or not things are going great, his self-confidence remains strong and high.

Even after writing this book, my feelings of self-confidence don't stay the same. However, my personal self-confidence is strong enough to realize that even if this book is imperfect, it still can be beneficial to many people who read it.

I plan to reread this book a number of times. Even though I wrote it, my self-confidence does fluctuate. Rereading certain sections already helped me gain perspective and strengthen my feelings of self-confidence when I needed a boost.

Normal people don't always feel self-confident. Even role models of self-confidence might have health challenges, financial challenges, success challenges, and many other forms of challenges that lower their thoughts and feelings of self-confidence. When self-confidence has been integrated and internalized, it is easier to be resilient. We can learn to bounce back fairly quickly. We can rest up and feel renewed and vibrantly alive.

When we expect our level of self-confidence to fluctuate, we won't be overly surprised when we are not always on the same high level of self-confidence.

In *Gateway to Happiness* I wrote, "Don't be sad that you are sad." Here too, "Don't be upset to see that your self-confidence is temporarily down."

Realize that it wasn't really the situation or circumstance that lowered your self-confidence. Rather, your thoughts about what was happening caused your self-confidence to go down. Integrating and internalizing this awareness is life changing. So let's repeat it: "Realize that it wasn't really the situation or circumstance that lowered your self-confidence. Rather, your thoughts about what was happening caused your self-confidence to go down."

Be resilient! Right this moment you are not in any past moment. You are here and now. You are reading about self-confidence rising and falling. Right now, allow your self-confidence to return to its highest level. If that is difficult at this very moment, at least you can reflect on what it would be like if you increased your self-confidence.

With the miraculous gift of imagination you can imagine how wonderful and marvelous it would be for your self-confidence to rise and be strong. Imagine a future moment when you will allow yourself to be highly self-confident. Self-confidence doesn't need perfection or intellectual brilliance. It doesn't need tremendous skills and talents. It just needs a mindset and attitude that your value as a person of immense worth is a birthright. You were valuable on your first day of life and you maintain that intrinsic value. Your feelings of self-confidence may rise and fall, but your value is constant.

Many people are relieved to know that most people don't experience steady levels of self-confidence, even those who truly have high levels of self-confidence. Be patient. A temporary drop in your self-confidence doesn't mean that it's gone. It's just temporary. And when you feel better, your self-confidence will go up again.

Someone told me, "I guess I'm a bit unusual when it comes to self-confidence. My self-confidence depends on who I am with at the time.

"There are some people who are considered great for very valid reasons. When I'm in their presence I feel their spirituality and their self-confidence rub off on me. My mind works at a high level when I talk to them. I think more clearly and I am more creative.

"On the other hand, there are other people in whose presence I feel much more limited. My mind does not work as well as it usually does. I haven't figured out the exact reason for this. I have learned to accept these fluctuations.

"Whether or not I clarify the dynamics of these higher and lower levels of self-confidence, my immediate goal is to appreciate the higher levels of self-confidence and to gracefully accept the lower levels. I hope that over time my mind will be able to function at its best, regardless of whose presence I am in."

55

YOU'RE ONE OF A KIND

No one in the world is exactly like you. You have a unique genetic makeup. You have a unique life history. Only you have your memories. Only you have the specific thoughts that constantly flow through your mind. Therefore your self-confidence is unique. No one else will have the exact same patterns of high and low self-confidence.

You are not in a self-confidence competition with anyone else. Unless you are a parent, teacher, mentor, coach, or someone who wants to help others improve their self-confidence, you don't need to know when anyone else's self-confidence is high and when it is low.

Instead of feeling bad because you think someone is more self-confident than you are, you can tell yourself, *Just as this person has developed his self-confidence, I can keep on developing my self-confidence.* You can learn from the self-confidence of others to become more self-confident.

Some people give an impression of being more self-confident than they actually are. Others appear less self-confident than they feel. Without entering his mind, you don't really know the ups and downs of anyone else's self-confidence. You would need to follow all his many thoughts and feelings to know the reality of someone else's self-confidence.

In some ways you probably are more confident than a specific person, and in other areas that person is more confident than you.

Your authentic self-confidence is unique. Because you are reading this book now and are reflecting on self-confidence, we can assume that you are on the path to greater self-confidence than someone similar to you who hasn't read the book and isn't interested in reading it. Notice the words, "similar to you." That phrase means the two of you have similar levels of intelligence, education, skills, and talents, and any other important area of life.

If you feel more self-confident every time you read "self-confidence," then rereading this book can help even more. It might not be noticeable to anyone else, but your mind registers this minuscule increase. You can allow yourself to feel good just knowing this.

"I used to think that I was very self-confident," someone told me. "I was innovative and creative. I could speak up and manage well, even in challenging situations that many others could not handle as competently.

"But then my self-confidence took a major turn downward. I lost the job I had for many years because the company went bankrupt. I quickly found a new job, but I soon found out that there were many duties in my new job that I wasn't confident about.

"I'm puzzled. Am I really self-confident or not?" this fellow wondered.

I replied, "You are similar to most people. Even the most successful people in the world have their areas of self-confidence and areas of lack of self-confidence. You are sincerely and authentically self-confident in your areas of strength and experience. There are many other areas where you are not confident.

"Keep building your competence in the areas that will be most beneficial for you. Find people who have strengths in areas that you don't, and find ways to benefit from their knowledge, skills, and strengths. They will gain from your strengths and you will gain from theirs."

"This conversation has really eased my mind," the fellow sighed in relief.

56

HEAR HASHEM RESPOND, "AND I LOVE YOU"

People who have had low self-esteem for a long time have developed the habit of looking in a mirror and saying, *I love you*. Some found this very difficult at first. But with practice, it became easier and easier. Eventually they found that their entire lives were transformed.

I never met my Zaidy Zelig, who had studied in Volozhin Yeshivah. He used to say, "I love You, Hashem *Yisbarach*," and would "hear" Hashem respond, "And I love you, Zelig." My father was very young when he had to say *Kaddish* for his father. But my Zaidy Zelig's impact on my father was very powerful.

My father frequently expressed his love for Hashem even in very challenging situations. My father's two great teachers, the Chofetz Chaim and his student Rabbi Yosef Kahaneman, founder and head of Ponevez Yeshivah, were role models of love for Hashem and loving kindness for other people. The

Chofetz Chaim wrote in his classic book, *Shemiras Halashon*, "The Almighty loves each person more than each person loves himself."

A person can gain so much self-confidence from expressing his love for Hashem *Yisbarach* and "hearing" the Creator and Sustainer of the universe saying in return, "And I love you." This will be helpful even without saying one's name. But those who have done this have found that it works even better when you add your own name.

Every time you touch a *mezuzah*, think, *I love You, Hashem Yisbarach, my Father, my King, Creator and Sustainer of the universe.* Imagine hearing the response, "And I love you [*your name*]."

You don't need to imagine how much you can benefit from this habit. You can try it out for free for the next 30 days. You don't even need to touch the *mezuzah*; you can just look at one. If you find this beneficial, you can try it out for an entire year and can keep up this habit for as long as you want. People have found this experiment to be incredibly helpful.

When we increase our love and gratitude for our Creator and Sustainer, our self-confidence increases. We were put in this world for a meaningful mission. Throughout our lives our unique mission becomes clearer to us.

> *The Chofetz Chaim once sent my father to Grodno on a mission to convince the Jewish owners of a factory to keep the factory closed on Shabbos. When my father later reported his conversation to the Chofetz Chaim, the Chofetz Chaim patted my father on the cheek and commented, "So young and so clever."*
>
> *The fact that the Chofetz Chaim had confidence in my father's*

ability helped my father have the self-confidence to succeed. The fact that we are alive means that our Creator believes in our ability to fulfill our life's mission. Let this knowledge strengthen our own self-confidence.

57

YOUR POWER TO PRETEND

To develop a positive trait that you don't yet have, speak and act in ways that are consistent with that positive trait. This is what the Rambam tells us to do in his classic work *Yad Hachazakah: Hilchos Dei'os* (Chapters 1 and 2). Some people are able to just start speaking and acting that way. Others find it difficult because they don't feel that it is "real" for them.

Many people have overcome this imaginary block by using the power of pretending. All young children are experts at pretending. You were once a young child so you too were able to do this. That means that if you are really motivated to practice pretending, you can start right now or at least by tomorrow or next week. The problem with next week is that it takes an entire week to get there and by then you might forget to pretend to be self-confident. So it's wise to start right now, or later today.

It might be easier to pretend to be self-confident if you can imagine being self-confident.But even if you can't mentally see yourself doing it, you can pretend to speak and act with self-confidence.

If someone challenges you by saying, "I don't think that you really are self-confident right now. I think you are just pretending to be self-confident," what can you say to that accusation? You can choose to be truthful. "Yes, you're right. I'm just pretending to be self-confident right now. And I'm assuming that if I keep it up, it will become real."

The person who challenged you may admire and respect you for your honesty. Or he might say, "I don't like the idea of speaking and acting self-confident if you don't really feel self-confident."

Then you have a choice. You might say, "I don't want to gain your disapproval so instead of pretending, I will hope for a miracle. Maybe one day I'll wake up and suddenly I'll really and actually and authentically be self-confident." Or you might choose to respond, "I agree; authentic self-confidence is better than pretend self-confidence. But since at this very moment I'm not feeling self-confident and I know that I can pretend to be more self-confident, I feel it's wiser to pretend. This way I can gain many of the practical benefits of self-confidence even before I have made it my natural and automatic way of being."

Many great people throughout history have accomplished great things by pretending to be more self-confident than they actually were. And many people did not speak and act the way they would have if they had just pretended to be self-confident. Most people have never heard of them. They did not accomplish or achieve and reach their potential. They were afraid of disapproval, or maybe they didn't believe that they could overcome imaginary hurdles and obstacles with just pretending, so they let those obstacles stop them.

Ignoring the power of pretending raises the risk of limiting your own accomplishments and achievements. Utilizing the great power of pretending increases your chances of benefitting yourself and many other people. Which choice will your personal history report?

When you pretend long enough to be self-confident, your self-confidence will grow and develop until you won't have to pretend anymore.

Someone told me, "My problem is that I'm not self-confident."

I replied, "Are you really not self-confident, or are you just pretending to be not self-confident?"

"Why would I pretend to be not self-confident?" the puzzled fellow asked.

"I don't know," I said. "But what if the only reason you are saying that you aren't self-confident is because you have been pretending for so long that you actually believe that you aren't self-confident?"

The fellow laughed out loud, "That would be ridiculous."

"I'm glad to hear that you don't want to do something that would be ridiculous," I said. "For the next few days, pretend that you are tremendously self-confident. Since you are only experimenting, you don't need to be certain that this will work for you. It would be ridiculous not to try this out because it might help you greatly."

He experimented and his self-confidence improved beyond his wildest imagination. Try it yourself; it might work for you also.

58

THE POWER OF SELF-CONFIDENT AFFIRMATIONS

Those who understand the true power of affirmations know that positive affirmations create every positive human trait and state of mind. Affirmations that confirm negative ideas create every negative trait and state. Will the power of your thoughts create joy or sadness; serenity or stress; love or hate; or kindness and compassion or apathy and indifference? Will your affirmations build courage or cowardice, or inner strength or weakness? Will your affirmations create hope or hopelessness?

What is an affirmation? Every word we say and every thought we think is essentially an affirmation.

People who tend to worry say and think worry-producing affirmations. People who tend to get angry easily and frequently only do so because of the affirmations they think and say. Joyful people benefit from the patterns of their words and thoughts. People who aren't yet self-confident might not yet realize that they lack self-confidence because of their habitual affirmations. Very self-confident people talk to themselves in ways that enable them to be self-confident. Some do it so automatically that they don't consciously think about being self-confident.

Anyone who wants to increase his self-confidence would be wise to consciously utilize the great power inherent in self-confident affirmations.

Many people have found that placing written affirmations where they will frequently see them has helped them remember to repeat similar messages.

Realizing that you are already subconsciously thinking and saying affirmations can help motivate you to consciously change your pattern of thought and speech. In the beginning the change may take effort. After a while no effort is needed. Positive affirmations become totally natural.

The benefits of self-confident affirmations are worth the investment of time and energy.

Here is a list of twenty affirmations to increase self-confidence. Be patient. You might have to review them many times before you automatically think similar thoughts.

- *I am tremendously self-confident.*
- *My self-confidence becomes stronger and stronger all the time.*
- *I benefit greatly from being self-confident and it enables me to help more people in more ways.*
- *Authentic self-confidence is my birthright and it goes together with a natural and authentic humility.*
- *Any imaginary block that holds back my self-confidence has permission to melt away.*

- *Every self-confident person I encounter serves as a role model to allow me to increase my self-confidence.*
- *Anyone I encounter who lacks self-confidence is a reminder to let my self-confidence flow forth, and, if possible, to say something to enhance this person's self-confidence.*
- *All infants have innate self-confidence and I was once an infant.*
- *My Creator is perfect. I am not. Lack of self-confidence would be an obstacle to fulfilling my true mission in life. I let all obstacles to my self-confidence melt away.*
- *My own thoughts created my insecurity. I am grateful for having been gifted with a mind that thinks. I will utilize my mind wisely and I will think and speak in ways that enhance my self-confidence.*
- *Every moment of self-confidence that I have experienced throughout my life is with me always. I am allowing myself to feel what it feels like to be self-confident.*
- *Being nervous will not prevent me from saying and doing what I would say and do with self-confidence. Eventually that nervousness will melt away.*
- *I am tremendously grateful to my Creator. A mind full of gratitude is free from the thoughts that might create a lack of self-confidence.*
- *I pray for balanced and wise self-confidence. Because I want to utilize my self-confidence to fulfill my mission in life, I trust that my prayer will be fulfilled.*
- *Before I go to sleep at night, I imagine how my self-confidence will enhance my life and the lives of others.*
- *I become more aware of any lack of self-confidence in my life. I calmly and gently think thoughts that will enable my self-confidence to become stronger and stronger.*

- *If I ever temporarily lack self-confidence, I allow my self-confidence to return to my mind.*
- *If I ever need self-confidence that I haven't actually experienced, I will practice speaking and acting that way. This will have a positive influence on my life.*
- *I will think of people who have said things to me that enhanced my self-confidence. Remembering their words will allow me to experience more self-confidence now.*
- *I am eternally grateful for the gift of self-confidence. To express my gratitude, I will help others increase their self-confidence.*

59

INTERNAL PRESSURE

The more important something is, the more likely someone will feel pressure to take care of it. Many people assume pressure comes from what other people think and say. They think pressure is caused by deadlines and the amount of work they have to do. These people think external situations or circumstances cause people to be nervous, tense, or stressed.

People who maintain their calm self-confidence realize that feelings of pressure really come from their own thoughts and attitudes.

This is why different individuals might be in very similar situations yet react differently. One person feels totally overwhelmed and says, "That situation was overwhelming." Another person doesn't react as strongly; he finds it very stressful, but not overwhelming. Yet another experiences mild stress. He says, "It was a bit stressful." Another person has a great sense of humor and finds the whole thing funny. He says, "That was hilarious." Like a professional comedy writer, he finds the humor that others fail to see. Another person enjoys drama and excitement in his life and enjoys the opportunity to experience the fun that he craves.

Yet another person lives on a high level of spirituality and finds profound meaning in the challenging situation. Every challenge brings him closer to our Father, our King, Creator and Sustainer of the universe. He says, "The greater the challenge, the greater my feeling of spiritual elevation. Thank You, Hashem *Yisbarach*, for another opportunity to bring me closer to You."

Some people are naturally calmer than others. But with greater awareness that feelings of pressure come from inside our own minds and not from the outside, we will increase our own ability to maintain calm self-confidence. The knowledge that others have reached higher levels of awareness during stressful situations can serve as a role model for you.

Observe your own thoughts and feelings. Notice that you blame outside factors when you feel less calm and self-confident. Keep building the realization, *My calm self-confidence is up to me.*

If you experience pressure that reduces your calm state and self-confidence, repeat, *The real source of my feelings is in my mind. I will talk to myself in ways that enable me to become calm and relaxed and maintain a high level of self-confidence.* Repeat *Inner calm and high self-confidence* when you find yourself losing that state of being.

Your attitude toward these words creates the feeling of calm self-confidence. With practice, you can gain greater expertise in mentally controlling your state of mind.

By keeping your focus on constant improvement in a calm, self-confident manner, you will see progress. If you are not progressing as fast as you would like, perhaps a teacher, mentor, or coach can make suggestions. But only you are in charge of your inner mind. Let this inspire you to be the best you that you can be.

A man noted for his inner calm and serenity worked for an established firm that was considered an extremely high-pressure workplace. He was asked about maintaining his calm in such an environment.

He replied, "When I was a young man I felt it a great honor to be hired by such a distinguished firm. But soon after being hired, I was shocked to find out the health toll that working for this company was having on its employees. Heart attacks and strokes were common at a much younger age than for employees of similar companies. I definitely wanted to spend my most productive years here. But I wanted to be healthy, to live to a ripe old age, and to enjoy my retirement.

"I realized that it wasn't the work itself that caused so much stress. Employees had the bad habit of needlessly causing themselves such mental pressure. I made a strong resolution to create an inner calm self-confidence, regardless of how anyone else would react. I wasn't going to needlessly sacrifice my health.

"I had a more spiritual outlook than many coworkers, who were focused just on making more money at all costs. They failed to guard their health through proper eating, sleeping, and taking daily walks.

"Over the years I enjoyed sharing my attitude and my lifestyle with others. I considered my spiritual, physical, and emotional well-being to be a higher priority than earning more money. I've found that the more self-confident someone really was, the more eager he was to learn from me. Those who were more insecure felt that they needed to show others how hard they were working."

60

THE SELF-CONFIDENCE WORKSHOP AND RETREAT

In my imagination I visualized organizing a weeklong self-confidence retreat. This fun camp would gather over 100 participants for an entire week of self-confidence training and conditioning.

Now you can imagine attending my camp full of self-confident, friendly, cheerful participants. You are mentally prepared to enjoy the entire experience tremendously as you develop your own authentic self-confidence.

Everyone at the retreat speaks and acts with great self-confidence. No one is arrogant or conceited. No one boasts. But everyone is totally and thoroughly self-confident. Everyone wants everyone else to be totally and thoroughly self-confident. Everyone believes in the ability to live with authentic self-confidence. Everyone talks with modest self-confidence in a joyful and blissful way.

You see smiles on everyone's face, just as everyone sees your smiling face. You radiate kindness and sincerely care for the welfare of everyone else. You all want to help everyone attending the retreat to reach his loftiest and most cherished goals.

You are not concerned about anyone being judgmental of you for sounding overly self-confident. You don't needlessly limit the way you talk at this retreat. You believe that the sky is the limit, and there is no limit to what you can think of accomplishing and achieving.

There is no sense of competition at this retreat. Everyone is happy that they can be helpful in any way possible. So if you want to emulate what anyone else says or does, that person is thrilled to have the opportunity to help another participant of the retreat.

Spending an entire week at such a retreat might be difficult for many people to arrange. But a workshop or seminar of a few hours is easier to put together. And if you have enough self-confidence, you might get together with a few people and organize the actual event to help people increase their self-confidence.

When I tell people about this imagined retreat, those who relate to it are very excited and enthusiastic to think about such an event. "I would love to be part of such an experience," they say.

Other people think of all kinds of reasons why this retreat might not work out as I would expect.

"It's not real," some argue.

The funny thing is that those who limit their potential self-confidence are not being real. They use their imagination to limit themselves. As I have said many times, "Since all needless limita-

tions are only imaginary, imagination can break through and melt those needless limitations."

"But I'm not very creative or imaginative," some people claim.

The good news is that you don't need to be creative or imaginative to think about this suggestion for improving your self-confidence. By reading this chapter you have already thought about it, regardless of whether or not you think it is a great idea.

There is no valid reason for not having self-confidence. If you can't actually achieve or accomplish something, reality will prevent it from happening. But most people really and truly have the potential to accomplish much more. Building self-confidence helps a person reach his potential.

61

CRITIQUING THE CRITIC

Kind and compassionate people have a strong desire to help others live a better life. They are happy when others accomplish and achieve. They would love to help make you even more successful. Their criticism might be motivated by love and caring for you. You can decide if the critique is valid.

If a person criticizes you in a negative way, you have a right to be critical of the way this person is criticizing you. If his criticism would be better received if he spoke in a more caring and compassionate way, he will thank you for pointing that out. If he loves to hear constructive criticism, he will be happy to receive your feedback.

If, however, he doesn't like to be criticized, then he has not reached the level of spiritual perfection that would enable him to love criticism. It might be wise not to mention these thoughts to him, but no one can stop you from thinking them. This realization might reduce the sting of what he is saying.

Great teachers and coaches always point out ways that their students can improve. The greatest among them do this in such a way that it's actually enjoyable and greatly appreciated.

If feedback sounds more like harsh criticism than truly caring and compassionate feedback, mentally review what the person said. Hear it being said in the tone of voice and choice of words that lift your spirits and joyfully motivate you to improve.

Keep in mind: You have a right to be self-confident even though you aren't perfect. Self-confidence is an attitude that everyone has a right to have.

People who sincerely want to grow and develop know they aren't perfect and never will be. That knowledge doesn't stop them from constantly striving for improvement with a joyful sense of appreciation for life itself and for all of the kindnesses bestowed upon them by our benevolent Creator.

During a class, I mentioned that we can change our fear of criticism to love of feedback by appreciating every opportunity to keep growing and improving ourselves.

A week later one of the attendees told me, "I used to shudder whenever I heard the word 'criticism.' I grew up in a home where I was constantly criticized. The tone of voice sounded harsh and angry. To this day I have a negative reaction from hearing anyone speaking in that tone of voice, even if they are talking to someone else. I'm not a young boy anymore, but the trauma of angry criticism has been with me my entire life – until now.

"What you said about appreciating feedback made total sense to me. You mentioned that a presidential candidate hires advisers to coach him on his public speaking. They tell him what he is doing

wrong and what he needs to do to improve. He even pays them to do this. This was an 'aha!' moment.

"I'm still far from actually loving criticism, but it no longer scares me. My self-confidence has increased and I'm certain that it will keep increasing."

62

CONTINUE TO WORK, PRACTICE, AND IMPROVE

"I continue to work, practice, and improve" is the motto of self-confident people when they talk about any skill, talent, or ability that they would like to change.

They don't allow mistakes to derail them. They don't let failure stop them from getting up and continuing to get better. Regardless of the level they are presently on, their mind is focused on constant improvement.

It's not realistic to expect perfection. And it's not realistic to expect to be highly skilled without working on that skill. To be an expert in any area takes a lot of practice over a long period of time. People with natural talents may become highly proficient more quickly than those who aren't talented in those areas, but everyone needs to keep practicing to gain mastery.

Intelligent self-confidence includes the knowledge that every basic skill needs to be learned. And then we all need to keep practicing and improving to become a master at anything worthwhile.

Some of the greatest public speakers sounded simply awful when they first began speaking in public. Some of the most highly successful salesmen and fund-raisers were unsuccessful before they were trained and practiced the skill. Some of the most interesting and insightful teachers were boring when they first tried to teach. Some great scholars had difficulties understanding what they tried to study as they began their intellectual journey. Some great leaders initially didn't know how to motivate and inspire people. Some of the greatest musicians sounded awful when they first tried to play their famous instrument.

But all of these people and many others like them kept practicing and practicing and practicing. Their self-confidence gave them the motivation to continue. Others initially didn't have self-confidence that they would excel. But their fear of failure and their strong desire to gain minimal proficiency made them keep practicing. They surprised others and themselves with their excellence.

Don't give in to pessimistic thoughts. Just because you think, *I'm not good at this now, and I never will be good at it,* doesn't prove that you really can't gain the proficiency you would wish for. Pessimistic thoughts are another hurdle to overcome while trying to reach a goal.

Optimism is a positive quality. But like everything in life, it needs a wise balance. A person who is overly optimistic might think that he should become extremely skilled much faster than possible. This overoptimism can lead to pessimism regarding that skill, instead of the understanding that more practice is all that is required.

A strong will to improve can be more beneficial than natural talent. The motto "There is nothing that can stand in the way of a strong will" has been proven over and over again. In a sports game, the strong will to win is felt by both competitors. But there is no competition with anyone in character development or any other aspect of spiritual development. A strong will and the knowledge of how to proceed is all you need to keep making progress.

Choose an area in which you sincerely want to excel. Be totally dedicated and determined to continue practicing until you reach a level of expertise. This determination and focus does wonders for one's self-confidence.

63

IF THE ALMIGHTY HELPS YOU, YOU CAN DO ANYTHING

Throughout history, people who have accomplished great things in the Torah world have had an attitude of, "If the Almighty helps you, you can do anything."

Those who have internalized this attitude were models of humility and modesty despite their accomplishments. They realized that the Almighty gave them the ability to accomplish as much as they did.

One spiritually elevated person used to say, "The Almighty didn't just help me. He is the One Who actually did it all."

Be transformed by the awareness and realization that, "If the Almighty helps you, you can do anything." Plug into the ultimate power. The Creator and Sustainer of the universe can do anything. He can give you abilities that you didn't think you had. This realization helps you elevate yourself and your thinking. You expand your awareness of your capabilities.

Believing you can't do something has the power to stop you from doing it. This sentence is very disempowering and many believe it, so let's repeat it again: Believing you can't do something has the power to stop you from doing it. Instead, imagine how much you would gain by having the empowering attitude of, "If the Almighty helps me, I can do anything."

Repeat this message to yourself over and over again. As you do, you will find yourself doing more things that at one time you thought you couldn't do.

For many years I witnessed Rabbi Noah Weinberg, of blessed memory, motivate and inspire his students to continue to grow and to accomplish more.

Some students claimed they weren't bright enough. They weren't creative enough. They weren't strong enough. They weren't assertive enough. They weren't talented enough. They really thought that their claims were true.

When anyone would try to claim that he couldn't do something, Rabbi Weinberg would say in a fatherly tone of voice, "If the Almighty helps you, you can do anything." These inspired students became teachers and leaders.

64

SELF-CONFIDENT PEOPLE AREN'T ALWAYS RIGHT

While the main goal of this book is to help people become more self-confident, a cautionary note is needed. Don't always believe someone just because he sounds self-confident. Self-confidence is not proof that his opinions or claims are correct.

Statements that sound self-confident only show that the person feels confident or that he is able to look and sound self-confident. As we have pointed out, this can be a very beneficial state of being. But sounding confident isn't absolute proof that someone is right.

This is especially important if someone who sounds totally self-confident says something to you that is not helpful or beneficial. For example, someone may confidently tell you, "You lack self-esteem," or "You're not as self-confident as you seem."

This person might be totally self-confident that he is right. He might believe that telling people that they lack self-esteem will ultimately be beneficial. He might feel that if people know they lack self-esteem, they are on course to improving their self-esteem. Such comments often result in bad feelings. Many who hear such comments feel bad because of their self-talk about self-esteem.

Lack of self-esteem is a subjective, negative thought. The speaker could inspire you to feel better about yourself now and throughout your life. In a confident, caring tone he could say, "You have innate well-being and health, both mental and physical. The only thing that holds you back are needlessly negative thoughts. The good news is, you always have the free will to choose uplifting and inspiring thoughts. I believe in you and your abilities. I bless you that you should believe in yourself and your abilities."

Regardless of how self-confidently someone said those limiting statements to you, you can now increase your own self-confidence in your potential and abilities.

Don't allow someone's self-confidence in his personal opinion to override your ability to verify the information for yourself. Self-confidence can be a great quality to have. But it has limitations.

A person with authentic self-confidence will be a truth-seeker and will gladly acknowledge any mistakes and errors. He will be happy to have someone point them out to him.

Right now, imagine 100 of the greatest people in history telling you, "You are valuable and precious. You have been created in the Almighty's image and are a child of the Creator. You have awesome potential and can become the greatest 'you' possible."

Imagine bringing these compliments to yourself as a young infant. Imagine growing up with this awareness. Imagine living your future with this awareness. Imagine how great you would feel now if you had known that this is who you really are.

65
OVERCOMING FEAR

Fears can prevent a person from doing many positive things in life. But these fears are totally self-created in the laboratory of imagination. Therefore, a positive application of imaginary self-confidence can overcome the fears imagination created.

When you imagine yourself being able to say and do things that were difficult, they become easier to actually say and do. Even if you only imagine that you have self-confidence, what you want to say gets said. What you want to do gets done.

Many people claim that they can't possibly say or do things that are not really impossible to say or do. They just feel uncomfortable when they think of saying or doing those things. However, we have the ability to take action even though we feel uncomfortable. This realization opens up the door of opportunity. This awareness lets us do things that we previously thought we couldn't do.

The feeling of discomfort is just another perception of anxiety or fear. Some people might choose to allow those feelings to be a high, impenetrable wall that stops them from proceeding. Because you are improving your self-confidence, you may choose to imagine feeling the discomfort but not allow it to hold you back. You can choose a better feeling at any given moment.

Create the wonderful habit of choosing better feelings. Allow your feelings of discomfort to melt away and be replaced with comfortable feelings. From now on, whenever you want to say something or do something positive, you can choose great feelings that give you confidence to take action.

To overcome fears, choose from an unlimited menu of confidence-enhancing feelings:

Great courage can overcome great fears. But for many situations you don't need great courage, you only need a small amount of self-confidence. The mental victory over those limiting feelings can create a truly great feeling. When you confidently and courageously say or do something difficult, the very act can give you a wonderful feeling of inner strength.

You can also choose laughter. Laugh for a minute or two. You might remember something funny and laugh. Or you can just laugh at nothing. This skill is easy to practice. All little children have this skill; some adults have forgotten that they can laugh. But even adults can relearn how to do this. The ability to laugh even though nothing is funny is a great skill for overcoming needless blocks. Try practicing on your own or find someone who can show you how to do it.

You can imagine that you are a master at creating feelings of joy by recalling your favorite joyful moments. After you do this enough times, you won't need to imagine that you are a master; you will know from experience that you can do it.

Reducing the degree of the discomfort will make it easier for you to say and do more things. And each experience of choosing better feelings makes the next experience easier.

66
SELF-CONFIDENCE ENABLES YOU TO DO MORE ACTS OF KINDNESS

Some people are motivated if they know that they will personally benefit from change. But other people are more motivated to improve when they know that others will gain as well. They should realize that the more self-confident they are, the more acts of kindness they can do for more people.

A person with high levels of self-confidence knows that he can ask other people to join him in doing acts of kindness. Some acts of kindness cannot be done alone. Asking others for help widens the scope of positive things that he can accomplish.

You might not be able to host someone who needs a place to eat or stay, but you might know others who can. Having the self-confidence to ask will make you a partner in that kindness.

You might know someone who could help a friend looking for a job. Having the self-confidence to ask that person might be the connection your friend needs.

People with high levels of self-confidence are more likely to ask people, "Is there any way I can help?" Some people might say, "If you need anything, just let me know," but might not really mean it. When a self-confident person says this, his sincerity comes through and his offer of help is more likely to be accepted.

Ask yourself, *If I were more self-confident, what difficult acts of kindness would I be able to do?*

Visualize yourself doing one of those acts of kindness. Run this image through your mind a number of times.

Doing an act of kindness that needs self-confidence builds your self-confidence. You are emulating our Creator by being kind to one of His children.

Someone I knew well once said to me, "When I was younger there were many things I would have liked to do for others, but I felt that I couldn't do them. I didn't do similar things for myself and I assumed that this was just my personality and it wasn't my fault.

"But one day when I was reflecting on building my self-confidence, I realized the truth. With increased self-confidence I would easily be able to say and do things that I previously thought were impossible! When I said, 'I can't,' my limited self-confidence had caused me to think that way. Now it is easy for me to do many kind things for others. Many of my 'I can'ts' have been upgraded to, 'I can and I will.' And then I do."

67

MOMENTS OF INSPIRATION

During our moments of inspiration we feel higher, wiser, and more capable. During a moment of inspiration our self-confidence is at its highest. It is wise to take action when we feel this way. This feeling might not last, but our actions can have a lasting effect.

Sometimes we see what we might not ordinarily see and think in ways that we might not ordinarily think. Such moments of mental clarity can have a major impact on our lives. The life-changing insights we experience help us understand ourselves better. The flow of ideas may lead to positive changes and exceptional accomplishments.

Don't waste these moments. Don't let them flicker out like a matchstick flame that lights up for a short while and then fades away. At the very least, write down some of your thoughts. After those elevated feelings have passed, you can reread what you have written.

Some readers will have many memories of such moments of clarity. Others will have just a few, but they remain vivid in their minds. Even if you currently find it challenging to recall moments of inspiration, you can be on the lookout for future moments of inspiration. By being mentally prepared, you will find it easier to recognize those moments.

Some people think of ideas they would like to implement but they don't get around to doing them. The time never seems exactly right. But during future moments of inspiration they may feel highly motivated. Keep this in mind. Look forward to future moments of inspiration. Those moments are like a bolt of lightning in the darkness illuminating the direction you need to go. The progress you make in those moments might be extraordinary.

If you have been waiting for a breakthrough or hoping for a moment of inspiration that hasn't appeared, imagine what you would say and do if you did experience that moment of inspiration. Be patient.

Without actually experiencing a moment of inspiration, it could take longer to be inspired to take action in a practical way. With sufficient patience, eventually you will be able to achieve and accomplish.

68

"EVERYONE I MEET IS MY FRIEND, LIKES ME, AND WANTS TO HELP ME"

People who consistently feel insecure around others have very different thoughts and attitudes about other people than those with self-confidence. The thoughts and attitudes of insecurity are, *Other people are judging me. They are critical of me. They won't like me. They will think that I am inferior or that something is wrong with me. Other people make me nervous. I wonder why?*

On the other hand, people who are self-confident around others have the attitude, *Everyone I meet is my friend. People like me. I will be happy to help others any way I can, and I feel confident that others will be happy to help me.*

The first pattern creates nervousness, anxiety, and fear; thoughts of self-confidence create inner calm and a sense of security. When you believe that others will be friendly, that they like you and want to help you, you give off an energy of likeability. Your thoughts create your feelings. Your positive feelings will be mirrored by others.

My father had this attitude. We lived in an inner-city area that was considered a bit rough. But I remember walking with my father to his shul on Shabbos, and people from very different backgrounds would ask my father for blessings and prayers.

This concept has been expressed a long time ago by King Solomon in *Mishlei* (Proverbs) 27:19, "As in water, face to face, so too is the heart of one person to another." When you look at your reflection in a pond or a mirror, you see your expression. If you smile, you see a smile. If you frown, you see a frown. So, too, is true for the feelings of your heart. When you unconditionally feel good feelings about someone, they tend to reciprocate similar feelings.

When you see people as good friends, who like you and want to help you, you will find amazing results. Those who make this their natural, heartfelt experience are well liked by all.

It's important not to view this as a manipulative technique used just to get something from someone, like an insincere salesman. Those who do not honestly like the other person but offer an external smile and a forced friendly tone of voice might wonder why this technique isn't working for them. The answer is simple. King Solomon says in the verse, "So too is the heart of one person to another." If the heart is missing, the essential ingredient isn't there so of course this doesn't help.

Someone who heard a class I gave on this topic said to me after class, "I would love to be sincere and authentic. I truly want to view others as my friend. I want to like people unconditionally. I want to do what I can to help others. But I'm not yet holding there. I have been selfish and self-centered in the past. But now I realize how much I would gain by having a change of heart. What can I do?"

"I see how sincere you really are as you ask this. With a similar sincerity, be sincerely kind. Speak and act with kindness. The Rambam tells us that when you do many acts of kindness over time, then you actually develop this trait. As you make kindness your habitual way of thinking, speaking, and acting, you are on the path of viewing others as a good friend. Be patient. It might take time to integrate and internalize. But with persistence and perseverance, you will eventually succeed."

69

LIGHTEN UP

The third verse of the Torah is, "Let there be light." Before this statement from the Creator, there was only darkness. And then there was light. We still benefit from the light today. Without the energy of this light, we could not exist.

Every cell in our body is ultimately a manifestation of energy. The awareness of the energy of health and the energy of lack of health is a field that keeps growing even among traditional physicians.

Our emotions are a product of our biochemistry. Our minds create hormones associated with our thoughts; these hormones effect how we feel. This is true for positive emotions such as joy, love, and serenity, as well as negative emotions of stress, fear, anger, and distress. Healthy thoughts of gratitude, happiness, joy, kindness, love, and serenity produce healthy biochemistry in our brain and throughout all the cells in our body. Distressful thoughts produce hormones that are not conducive for our total well-being.

Allow yourself to imagine a calm and peaceful place. Breathe slowly and deeply. With each breath, you can repeat to yourself, *I am more and more relaxed with each and every breath. I am allowing myself to be totally in the present, and I'm becoming calmer and calmer. All my muscles are relaxing as my mind becomes more and more peaceful.*

As you begin feeling calmer and more relaxed, imagine a wonderfully healing white light traveling from head to toe, relaxing each and every muscle. This light has healing energy for all of your cells, and you feel more and more at ease and relaxed.

Keep this up for a few minutes. As you become more and more relaxed, imagine yourself becoming more and more self-confident. Imagine how you would look and sound if you were totally self-confident. Imagine how you would speak and what you would say as your self-confidence increases.

The more frequently you practice this, the more it becomes part of your consciousness. By sending soothing and relaxing light to every cell in your body and neuron in your brain, you create an inner calm. In your calm state, you will find it much easier to see, hear, and feel yourself speaking and acting with self-confidence.

> *Someone was habitually stressed by thinking about what went wrong in the past and what might go wrong in the future. He asked me for a practice that could help him be calmer and more self-confident. He wanted to find solutions to potential problems.*
>
> *I calmed him by telling him that daily repetition of the mental program will help him feel much better more often; he will also notice that his self-confidence gets stronger every day.*

I explained the mental program. Closing his eyes with the intention to imagine a calm and serene place would make it easier to visualize himself talking and acting with self-confidence. His stressed state was a distressed beta brain frequency. Calm self-talk with his eyes closed would easily slow his brain waves to a state known as alpha.

"As you close your eyes, repeat the words, 'Let there be light.' Repeat this slowly and with the self-assurance that as you practice this regularly, it will become easier. Feel all your muscles relaxing. Say to yourself, 'I allow all my muscles to relax as I repeat, "Let there be light."'

"When you feel your muscles relaxing, imagine being blessed with solid and modest self-confidence. Right now, in your mind, you are creating the thoughts and feelings that you want to think and feel. Your mind is yours and you can choose to mentally practice being the way you wish to be. Because of this practice, your self-confidence will be there for you whenever you wish. Now hear your inner voice repeating, 'My self-confidence will enable me to be the way I wish to be whenever I say "self-confidence."'

"You can imagine real-life situations when you will have self-confidence, or you can use your imagination to imagine the most extreme situations and see yourself speaking and acting with total self-confidence. Feel the joy of knowing how great this will feel. You can have these same feelings whenever you choose to close your eyes and say, 'Let there be light.' Using a joyful tone of voice will add a greater spiritual and emotional dimension of joy. As you notice the sun shining its light on the world, you will have greater appreciation for all that the Creator has done for you throughout your life.

"You can decide how long each session will last. You might want to make this a frequent two-minute practice. Or when you are faced with challenges where greater self-confidence will help you find solutions, you can practice for 20 minutes. You will feel calmer and more relaxed each time you practice. As soon as you are ready, you can count from one to five and wake up with more self-confidence.

"As you notice how self-confident you are becoming, you will recognize that you are now a very self-confident person. You think self-confidently, you speak self-confidently, and you act self-confidently. You created this confidence in your own mind and it became your everyday reality.

"Over time, you will surprise yourself with your great feelings as you become more and more self-confident in more and more situations."

Dear reader, I know from personal experience that this works well for anyone who is patient and persistent. You can record this mental conditioning and replay it so it becomes integrated in your own mind. Some people might want to hear their own voice repeating these words. Others might ask someone who sincerely wants them to become calmer and more self-confident to record this exercise for them.

70

GREAT THOUGHTS, FEELINGS, WORDS, AND ACTIONS CREATE A GREAT LIFE

When you make it a habit to think great thoughts, say great words, and do great things, you feel great more and more often. Your self-confidence skyrockets!

Don't try to be perfect. Perfectionism creates a lot of needless stress. It certainly doesn't lead to anyone being perfect. Learn from others, but don't compare yourself with anyone else. The greatest people in the world were great because of their thoughts, words, and actions. Emulating those people will put you on a path to creating a better and higher life. Your great thoughts, great words, and great actions are unique to you.

Appreciate progress. True greatness takes an entire lifetime, but we live our lives one moment at a time. We live one day at a time. One week at a time. One month at a time. They add up to one year at a time.

Our individual moments of great thoughts, words, and actions add up. We don't have to choose great thoughts all at once; we only have to choose our next thought. Therefore, it's one great thought at a time. The same applies to words and actions. We only need to choose our next word and our next action. One great word at a time and one great action at a time add up to a great life.

When I teach this formula in workshops and classes I have everyone chant: "Great thoughts create great feelings. This leads to great words and great actions. And all this creates a great life."

Let's repeat it: Great thoughts create great feelings. This leads to great words and great actions. And all this creates a great life.

Chanting this enthusiastically with a joyful tone of voice has a positive effect on your mind and body. Repeating it many times strengthens the neural pathways in your brain and makes it easier to think in these terms more easily. This creates upbeat feelings and makes it easier to choose positive words and take positive actions.

You can choose to use this affirmation, *I think great thoughts more and more often. I feel great feelings more and more often. I speak great words more and more often. I take great actions more and more often.*

If you don't want to repeat this out loud, just let these words reverberate in your mind: *Great thoughts create great feelings. This leads to great words and great actions. And all this creates a great life.*

At times it might be more realistic to say, *Better thoughts create better feelings. This leads to better words and better actions. And all this creates a better life.*

Eventually you might feel so much better that you will feel like saying, *Awesome thoughts create awesome feelings. This leads to awesome words and awesome actions. And all this creates an awesome life.*

Just reading this one time adds this concept to your mental library. It is stored in your subconscious for the rest of your life. Repetition puts this powerful message at the forefront of your conscious mind. If you want this positive pattern to be internalized and integrated, it is wise to keep repeating: *Joyful thoughts create joyful feelings. This leads to joyful words and joyful actions. Keep this up to create a joyful life.* The more frequently you repeat it, the easier it will be for you to consciously think these thoughts.

Before you fall asleep at night, you can repeat to yourself: *Great thoughts create great feelings. This leads to great words and great actions. And all this creates a great life.*

If you have a difficult time falling asleep, instead of counting sheep, repeat this mantra in a tired and sleepy tone of voice. This will calm your mind and will help you relax. It's a great meditation. You can even choose to repeat, *Calm thoughts create calm feelings. This leads to calm words and calm actions. And this creates a calm life.*

When you wake up in the morning, after expressing your gratitude for being given another day of life, you can remind yourself, *Great thoughts create great feelings. This leads to great words and great actions. And all this creates a great life.* This can help you start off your day in a great way.

You can share this mantra with young children. If you repeat it in an upbeat tone of voice, the energy in your voice will lift their spirits. Even if they are not yet old enough to understand the ramifications of the words, these words will program and condition their minds. The long-term effects will be tremendously beneficial.

If no one told you this encouraging thought when you were a child, realize that you can say it to yourself. Some people like to imagine meeting themselves when they were younger and sharing these words of encouragement. Other don't have to use this as a retroactive technique. They instead imagine thinking, speaking, and acting in great ways in the future and benefit in the present.

I bless you to think great thoughts, to have great feelings, to speak great words, and to take great actions. Then you will automatically live a great life.

"My life has been a total mess," the fellow complained. "I've suffered from my negativity for so long that I don't have any hope of improving my life."

"If you knew that people in much worse shape than you totally transformed their lives, could you accept such a transformation is possible for you, too?"

He had to agree that this makes sense.

I told him, "I met someone who volunteered in a high-security prison. The inmates had committed serious crimes and thought that nothing could change them. But this extremely kind and compassionate elevated spiritual master believed in the sanctity of the inner soul of even these hardened criminals. Their hearts would eventually melt, because he refused to give up on them. His belief in them was stronger than their own disbelief in themselves."

At first this fellow argued that he couldn't change his thinking. I agreed that as long as he wanted to prove that he couldn't improve his thinking and his life, this would be his reality. But if he was willing to experiment with the power of realizing that the quality of his thoughts created the quality of his life, he would see great progress in a much shorter time than he imagined.

I persisted until he acknowledged my point. Although a major change took longer than he had hoped it would, he did see remarkable progress right away. The direction of improvement is more important than speed. The essence is in knowing the power of your personal thinking to create your life.

71

CONFIDENTLY STOP GOSSIP

It takes self-confidence to stop people from speaking *lashon hara* [negative gossip]. As you increase your self-confidence it will be easier to tactfully and diplomatically convey the message that this type of communication is wrong. If the speaker insists on continuing, you remain equally determined not to listen to it.

If you haven't yet developed the self-confidence to explain why to avoid this type of conversation, develop the skill of changing the subject. If someone starts to speak against another person, bring up another topic. People change the subject all the time in daily conversations.

If the speaker returns to the *lashon hara*, persist in talking about something else. You might say, "I just remembered a great story," and then start telling an inspiring or elevating story. If you can't think of one, talk about the wonders of creation, like Rabbi Avigdor Miller did. You might talk about eating healthful food to be healthier and live longer, just as *Shmiras Halashon* – being careful about what one talks about – leads to a longer life.

The more self-confident you are, the more ways you will be able to avoid hearing *lashon hara*. I once heard a congregant in my father's shul comment , "I have enough faults of my own, I don't need to hear about the faults of others." The speakers immediately changed the subject. This happened about 45 years ago, and it stuck in my mind because it is a great approach.

Be tactful. Be diplomatic. Find the kindest and most compassionate ways to influence people to care about the dignity and welfare of others. Help them refrain from needlessly speaking about the faults and shortcomings of others.

A fellow who was very careful not to speak lashon hara said to me, "I find it easy not to speak against other people. But I find it extremely difficult to tell others not to speak lashon hara in my presence. What can I do to make it easier?"

I told him, "I met someone who used to say, 'I feel good when I hear about the good things that people have done, and I feel bad if I happen to hear about something negative. Please help me feel good.' It's very effective when said in a friendly tone of voice."

72
ACCESS SELF-CONFIDENCE WITH PERSONALIZED TRIGGERS

Some people are self-confident day and night, in all seasons, in all situations, and with all people. Everyone else can use the power of making and using triggers, also known as anchors.

When you associate a sound, a sight, a movement, or a touch with a specific emotional state or feeling, you can access or "trigger" that state with a repetition of that anchor. This is also known as classical conditioning. The most famous example is the dog that salivated when he heard the sound of a bell. The scientist, Ivan Pavlov, repeatedly gave the dog its favorite food and rang a bell when it was excited about the food. When he rang the bell later, the dog salivated even if there was no food. The bell acted as a trigger.

We all have many triggers. Some are positive. Some are negative. We have the ability to create a positive anchor to enable us to access high levels of self-confidence whenever we wish.

To create a self-confidence anchor, wait until you feel a high level of self-confidence, or use your imagination and act as if you were totally and intensely self-confident. At the height of that state, press your thumb and the next two fingers together. Say or think, *High levels of self-confidence.* Repeat this phrase a number of times and you will have established this motion as a trigger to access self-confidence.

Some people prefer to create this state by thinking of their most self-confident role model. When they imagine that they are this person and that they feel the way this person feels, they set their anchor. They repeat this a number of times. When they need to be in this state in the future, they apply their trigger image of their role model.

Some individuals find it easier to access their self-confident state at will. Others need to practice more. But every human being can be conditioned to respond to a self-confidence trigger. Those who feel that it's impossible need to do this the most.

If you can't trigger self-confidence on your own, it's worthwhile to make the effort to find someone who can show you how. Have the self-confidence that you will be able to do this on your own or that you will find a teacher or coach who can help you.

"When I first heard about making anchors to trigger positive states, I felt that this was superficial and not authentic," someone said to me. "I resisted the entire idea. I didn't want to have to do anything special to have self-confidence. I just wanted to be self-confident because that is how I really am.

"But then I realized that I was limiting myself greatly by not

being able to access the self-confidence that would help me personally, financially, and even spiritually.

"I often found it difficult to ask for what I wanted. Self-confidence would make it much easier. I didn't speak up when I felt I should. Self-confidence would enable me to speak up. I avoided certain people and certain situations. Self-confidence would enable me to interact with those people and I wouldn't need to avoid the situations that I previously avoided.

"In your class about creating more joy and having a greater amount of self-confidence, you explained the idea of making anchors. That's when I saw how real they are. It's a natural process that we all have spontaneously done many times in our lives without realizing it. Hearing the term 'self-confidence' had been triggering my resistance to becoming self-confident! I stopped being so stubborn about not consciously creating positive anchors. I am very grateful that I now have this tool in my mental toolbox."

73

MENTAL CONDITIONING THROUGH READING AND REVIEWING THIS BOOK

This book's basic message can be summarized in one sentence: You create self-confidence in your own mind with the thoughts that you consciously think.

That's it. Your self-confidence is an inside job. You only need to be self-confident when you need self-confidence. And whenever you need self-confidence, realize that you already have memories of self-confidence stored in your brain.

"So why do I need to read this entire book?" you might ask.

If you are already tremendously self-confident and maintain your self-confidence regardless of the situation, no matter what happens or what anyone says to you, you don't need to read this book for yourself. You might want it as an act of kindness for someone else. You might want to read it to someone who wouldn't read it on his own.

I find that my own level of self-confidence depends upon my emotional state at the moment. When I am well rested and in a state of well-being, I am self-confident. But when I am fatigued and hungry and in a challenging situation, I don't access my self-confidence as easily. I will be happy to have this book on my shelf so I can reread the ideas when I need a boost of self-confidence. I already know the concepts, but when they are at the forefront of my consciousness, it will be easier for me to access a self-confident state.

The purpose of this book is not to supply the reader with a lot of new ideas. Rather, the goal of this book is to help you strengthen the conditioning of your mind's ability to access a self-confident state.

Every time you review an idea, you strengthen your brain's neural pathways containing that idea. This is similar to strengthening a muscle by exercising it over and over again. Whenever you review an idea, there are actual physical changes going on in your brain. When I was a child, this information about an adult's brain wasn't known yet. With the advancement of brain technology, it has been seen clearly that brains that are exercised properly grow and develop. The changes are minuscule. You can't feel it happening. But you can clearly see the results over time in your thoughts and feelings.

Every time you read anything about your self-confidence getting stronger and stronger, your self-confidence gets stronger. The only condition is that you don't consciously argue or fight with this strengthening.

If you are doubtful that you can strengthen your self-confidence just by reading about it, test it out. But be fair to yourself. If you say to yourself, *I'll try it out just to prove that this won't work,* it really won't work. If you want to prove that you can't increase your self-confidence, you will successfully prove your point, to your detriment.

Since you are reading this book, it seems that you are sensibly assuming that self-confidence can be increased. Great! Be patient and prove yourself right. The more frequently you read these sections, the more you will strengthen your ability to enhance your self-confidence.

Dear Reader,

This chapter is the last chapter because it summarizes the entire message of this book. I have found that many readers like to look at both the first chapter and the last chapter before they read any other section of a book. If you have flipped to the end early, this conclusion is exactly what you need at this very moment.

If you read all the chapters from the beginning to the end, this summary of the entire book will serve you well on your continued journey of living a life of self-confidence.

I hope this book has increased your self-confidence. May you be a Divine messenger to help other people add to their self-confidence to accomplish many positive things throughout their lives.

Sincerely,
Rabbi Zelig Pliskin